# DOMESTIC VIOLENCE

Hedy Cleaver

**This book has kindly been supported with funding from the de Brye Charitable Trust.**

BAAF
ADOPTION
& FOSTERING

Published by
**British Association for Adoption & Fostering**
(BAAF)
Saffron House
6–10 Kirby Street
London EC1N 8TS
www.baaf.org.uk

Charity registration 275689 (England and Wales)
and SC039337 (Scotland)

British Library Cataloguing in Publication Data
A catalogue record for this book is available from the British Library

ISBN 978 1 910039 31 1

Project management by Shaila Shah, Director of Publications, BAAF
Designed and typeset by Fravashi Aga
Printed in Great Britain by the Lavenham Press
Trade distribution by Turnaround Publisher Services, Unit 3,
Olympia Trading Estate, Coburg Road, London N22 6TZ

BAAF is the leading UK-wide membership organisation for all those
concerned with adoption, fostering and child care issues.

# Contents

Looking behind the label…

Foreword                                                    vii
Polly Neate, CEO, Women's Aid Federation

## SECTION I
## THE IMPACT OF DOMESTIC VIOLENCE
## ON CHILDREN                                               I

   Introduction                                             3
1  The effects on parenting                                  7
2  Links with child abuse and neglect                       II
3  The impact on children under five years                  15
4  The impact on middle year children                       23
5  The impact on adolescence                                31
6  The challenge facing adoptive parents and foster carers   38

## SECTION II
## PARENTING CHILDREN AFFECTED BY
## DOMESTIC VIOLENCE                                          43

Can we break the cycle?                                      45
Helen Dunning

Inviting in the storm                                        67
Melinda Rigopoulo

References                                                   90
Useful organisations                                         93

## Notes about the authors

**Dr Hedy Cleaver** is an Emeritus Professor at Royal Holloway College, University of London. Her experience as a social worker and child psychologist informs her research on vulnerable children and families and the impact of professional interventions. The guiding principle underpinning her work is a desire to improve the quality of life for children living in circumstances that place them at risk of abuse and/or neglect. The findings from her research have had an identifiable impact on policy in the UK in respect of children and families over the last 25 years.

**Helen Dunning** writes: I work in a secondary school and I have responsibility for sixth formers with special educational needs to teach them life skills. As a mature student (I was previously a hairdresser), I had many different jobs to pay the mortgage, but they all revolved around working with young people on the edges of society.

I looked into adoption as a first choice as a single woman in my thirties. I was brought up in a single parent family from my teens. Lee was placed as an older hard-to-place child and I've remained single to focus on his needs. I have found myself a large group of friends who are also adopters and meet up with them often.

**Melinda and Nikos Rigopoulo** and their two birth children adopted Luca, aged two, some 10 years ago. Both parents had professional experience of working with children and for the first two months after placement, both took time out to stay at home with Luca. Melinda subsequently used the whole year of adoption leave that she was entitled to, after which she returned to work part-time. They feel that this was the single best thing they ever did in the whole process!

## The series editor

The editor of this series, **Hedi Argent**, is an established author/editor for BAAF. Her books cover a wide range of family placement topics; she has written several guides and a story book for young children.

# Looking behind the label...

*Jack has mild learning difficulties and displays some characteristics of ADHD and it is uncertain whether this will increase...*

*Beth and Mary both have a diagnosis of global developmental delay...*

*Abigail's birth mother has a history of substance abuse. There is no clear evidence that Abigail was prenatally exposed to drugs but her new family will have to accept some kind of developmental uncertainty...*

*Jade has some literacy and numeracy difficulties, but has made some improvement with the support of a learning mentor...*

Prospective adopters and carers are often faced with the prospect of having to decide whether they can care for a child with a health need or condition they know little about and have no direct experience of. No easy task...

Will Jack's learning difficulties become more severe?
Will Beth and Mary be able to catch up?
When will it be clear whether or not Abigail has been affected by parental substance misuse?
And will Jade need a learning mentor throughout her school life?

It can be difficult to know where to turn for reliable information. What lies behind the diagnoses and "labels" that many looked after children bring with them? And what will it be like to live with them? How will they benefit from family life?

Parenting Matters is a unique series, "inspired" by the terms used – and the need to "decode" them – in profiles of children needing new permanent families. Each title provides expert knowledge about a particular condition, coupled with facts, figures and guidance presented in a straightforward and accessible style. Each book also describes what it is like to parent an affected child, with adopters and foster carers "telling it like it is", sharing their parenting experiences, and offering useful advice. This combination of expert information and first-hand experiences will help readers to gain understanding, and to make informed decisions.

Titles in the series deal with a wide range of health conditions and steer readers to where they can find more information. They offer a sound introduction to the topic under consideration and offer a glimpse of what it would be like to live with a "labelled" child. Most importantly, this series looks behind the label and give families the confidence to look more closely at a child whom they otherwise might have passed by.

Keep up with new titles as they are published by signing up to our newsletter on www.baaf.org.uk/bookshop.

Shaila Shah

Titles in this series include:

- *Parenting a Child with Attention Deficit Hyperactivity Disorder*

- *Parenting a Child with Dyslexia*

- *Parenting a Child with Mental Health Issues*

- *Parenting a Child Affected by Parental Substance Misuse*

- *Parenting a Child with Emotional and Behavioural Difficulties*

- *Parenting a Child with Autism Spectrum Disorder*

- *Parenting a Child with Developmental Delay*

- *Parenting a Child with or at risk of a Genetic Disease*

# Foreword

This book is important for anyone placing children for adoption, supporting adoptive parents, or considering adoption themselves.

The impact of domestic violence on children and young people who live with it is devastating and long term. If their need for specialist support to recover is overlooked, those experiences will cast a dark shadow for years to come. This important book makes it abundantly clear that no matter how safe from future abuse, even if adopted, there is no short cut to recovery. Yet many agencies carry on as though there were.

Adoption presents significant challenges for many parents, and the harsh reality of parenting a child who has experienced domestic violence is a far from uncommon experience. The stories in this book are also a timely reminder that it is more often the child's own mother who must attempt to repair the damage, while also recovering herself from a life of constant fear, extreme danger and utter disempowerment. Domestic violence and abuse can severely undermine a woman's ability to parent confidently and safely. Specialist domestic violence services have amassed over 40 years' experience in recovery for mothers and children together, both in safe accommodation and in the community, but this lifeline is being cut for many women and children as funding is withdrawn from these services by local authorities. Yet in these same local authorities, children's departments depend on specialist domestic violence services as a means of ensuring children's safety.

Instead of support, mothers experiencing domestic violence more often receive threats and blame from professionals. It is common for a woman to be presented with a deadline to leave the perpetrator or her children will be removed. If she leaves him, she may then be told that she must facilitate contact between the children and the perpetrator, a man who was previously considered too dangerous for them to live with. A Women's Aid survey in 2013 found that 35 per cent of children in refuges who had themselves directly been abused by the perpetrator were still in contact with him.

A third of referrals to refuges are now refused because of lack of space. In some areas, only women who are defined as "high risk" having reported to the police (which most do not) will be offered support, but only to see them through the criminal justice process. It is hardly surprising that recovery and independence remain a distant goal for many, with re-victimisation, drug and alcohol misuse, mental health problems and homelessness a constant danger; the removal of their children may follow later, when they are even more vulnerable.

If we are to support children who have lived with domestic violence better, we must support their mothers.

All this, of course, is no help for women and men who adopt severely traumatised children and then find – just as their birth mothers did – that, tragically, love is just not enough. The stories of adoptive parents in this book are stories of extraordinary resilience, resourcefulness and hope: a timely reminder of the support desperately needed by all those parenting in the aftermath of domestic violence and abuse.

**Polly Neate**
Chief Executive, Women's Aid Federation

# UNDERSTANDING THE IMPACT OF DOMESTIC VIOLENCE ON CHILDREN

HEDY CLEAVER

# Introduction

Domestic violence is linked strongly to child abuse and neglect.
It is present in over half of all child protection cases coming to
the attention of the NSPCC and identified in a similar proportion
of local authority cases that result in care proceedings being
undertaken. Consequently, many carers and adoptive parents will
be confronted with children whose challenging behaviour has its
roots in domestic violence. An understanding of the impact of
domestic violence on children's health, emotional and behavioural
development will enable carers and adoptive parents to work
more effectively with their children. The information presented
in this section is based on research carried out by the author
(Cleaver *et al*, 2011).

## What is domestic violence?

Domestic violence, also referred to as domestic abuse and

3

interpersonal violence, should not be thought of solely in terms of physical and sexual assaults. It covers a much broader range of behaviours involving the abuse of power, defined by the Home Office (2013) as:

> *Any incident or pattern of incidents of controlling, coercive, threatening behaviour, violence or abuse between those aged 16 or over who are, or have been, intimate partners or family members regardless of gender or sexuality. The abuse can encompass, but is not limited to:*

> *psychological*
>
> *physical*
>
> *sexual*
>
> *financial*
>
> *emotional*

> *Controlling behaviour is a range of acts designed to make a person subordinate and/or dependent by isolating them from sources of support, exploiting their resources and capacities for personal gain, depriving them of the means needed for independence, resistance and escape and regulating their everyday behaviour.*

> *Coercive behaviour is an act or a pattern of acts of assault, threats, humiliation and intimidation or other abuse that is used to harm, punish, or frighten their victim.*

4

The law in relation to domestic abuse may strengthen following the Home Office consultation, which concluded on 15 October 2014 (Home Office, 2014).

Domestic violence is not confined to any particular group in society but crosses all religious, class and "race" barriers. It is also not confined to heterosexual relationships and may take place in lesbian, gay, bisexual and transgender relationships and can involve other family members, including children. Thus, children from all walks of life may experience domestic violence.

It is also widespread: over a third of people report that they have experienced some form of domestic violence (abuse, threats or force), sexual victimisation or stalking. A minority, largely women, suffer multiple attacks, severe injuries, and experience a range of inter-personal violence that is highly disruptive to their lives. We don't know how many children grow up in families where such behaviour is commonplace because children and families are often ashamed of their circumstances and reluctant to tell anyone what is happening. Recent work by the NSPCC would suggest that some 12 per cent of children under the age of 11 years and 18 per cent of those aged between 11 and 17 years have experienced domestic violence (Radford et al, 2011).

Women are far more likely than men to be the victims of domestic violence. As a result, the majority of children living in violent households will have witnessed the abuse of their mother. Domestic violence, however, does not always follow the pattern of male aggressor and female victim. Women can be responsible for the violence and mutual violence is not uncommon. Thus, children may have seen their father, or father figure, being victimised or witnessed the aggression of both parents. When violence does occur, mutual or otherwise, women are more likely to be seriously injured or killed following an assault, than are men.

SECTION 1

5

Domestic violence rarely exists in isolation. Many birth parents in these situations also misuse drugs and alcohol, experience poor physical and mental health, have a history of childhood abuse and have grown up in care. For example, half the men who perpetrate domestic violence have an alcohol problem and a fifth are depressed (Cleaver *et al*, 2011). In contrast, the impact of being subjected to domestic violence leaves many women with mental health difficulties, and in order to cope they may take prescription medicines or use drugs and/or alcohol. The co-morbidity of issues compounds the difficulties birth parents experience in meeting the needs of their children, and increases the likelihood that the child will have been abused and neglected.

## What all children need

When examining the impact of domestic violence on parenting capacity, it will help us understand how it can affect children's safety and welfare if we keep in mind what all children need to reach their full potential.

> To thrive, all children need love, adequate nutrition, sleep, warmth and to be kept clean.

> To become securely attached, they need emotional warmth and positive responses from their parents.

> To develop their full potential, they need adequate and appropriate stimulation and adults who believe in them.

> Children also need to be valued for themselves; they need to feel that they come first in their parents' lives.

> Finally, children need the support and encouragement to overcome the challenges life will throw at them.

# CHAPTER 1

# The effects
# on parenting

The likelihood that mothers will be the targets of domestic violence and are at risk of serious injury impacts on children to a greater extent than when fathers are the targets. The abuse of the mother places children at risk of abuse and neglect because domestic violence can have a profoundly negative effect on her capacity to look after or protect her children, and the role of parenting in the majority of families remains the responsibility of the mother.

The mother's ability to look after her children will be affected by the severity of the violence she experiences. Domestic assaults can take the form of slapping, punching, kicking, burns and stabbing, sexual abuse and rape, with the consequences of black eyes, bruising, broken bones and, in the most extreme cases, death.

*He tried to get her to drink the bleach, to pour it in her mouth whilst he held her there, and when he*

7

*couldn't make her, he poured bleach all over her face and hair. He was trying to kill her.*
(Mullender *et al*, 2002, p 94)

Domestic violence is rarely confined to physical or sexual assaults but involves a mixture of physical and psychological violence. Emotional abuse, such as constant criticism, undermining and humiliation may have a profoundly negative effect on the parent's mental health. It can result in a loss of confidence, depression, feelings of degradation, problems with sleep, increased isolation and the frequent use of medication and alcohol – all factors that impact on the capacity to look after children adequately.

The parent's self-confidence may be affected by having been belittled and insulted in front of the children. Such experiences will not only undermine self-respect, but also the authority needed to parent confidently. A parent's relationships with the children may also be affected because, in attempting to placate her (or his) partner and avoid further outbursts of violence, the abusive partner's needs are prioritised over those of the children. This preoccupation with trying to control the domestic environment may result in the violated parent becoming emotionally distant, unavailable or even abusive to the children.

Depression is a common reaction to domestic violence with the classic symptoms of apathy and listlessness and difficulty in organising day-to-day living. This may mean that the birth parent reacts in unpredictable, inconsistent and ineffective ways. When the family lifestyle is disorganised, rituals such as birthdays get forgotten or disrupted; planning becomes very difficult, as does the maintenance of familiar routines, such as meal or bedtimes and getting children ready for school. Domestic violence and the consequent depression may cause parents to be irritable and angry or withdrawn. As a result they could have difficulty in being emotionally available and affectionate with their children. When a parent becomes withdrawn and preoccupied by her (or his) own needs, the child's cues for attention may be missed. The effects of domestic violence on a parent's mental health may also result in the child's physical needs being neglected. Perhaps of greatest concern is that all these issues pose a real risk to the process of attachment and to relationships generally between children and their parents. The failure to develop secure attachment patterns early in life may mean that children have developed shaky internal working models, which can have adverse consequences for later relationships.

The social lives of children who have lived with domestic violence are often very restricted. Mothers or fathers who are subjected to violence, in all its forms, find it extraordinarily difficult to reveal what is happening to them because they are ashamed. They may also be reluctant to talk about their circumstances because they are afraid that their immediate family and friends will lack understanding and judge them. A parent may keep silent about their situation through fear of her (or his) partner's violence. The ability to make close friendships or keep in touch with family members may be compromised because of the control exerted over them. For example, the abuser may withhold access to the phone and to transport, undermine personal relationships, constantly "check-up" or accompany, or even subject the abused to imprisonment. As a result, the abused parent and the children may become isolated from all support.

All these issues impact on parents' capacity to meet the developmental needs of their children. To grow up in a violent household may result in the children failing to thrive because they do not receive the love they need, adequate nutrition, sleep, and warmth. Domestic violence also influences how parents relate to their child and impacts on the attachment between child and parent. The helplessness and hostility that are associated with

9

domestic violence and depression may interfere with the ability to be a warm and consistent parent. Birth mothers who have previously provided sensitive and competent parenting may be unable to do so after the arrival of a violent partner.

Children may fail to develop their full potential because when parents are subjected to domestic violence they are unable to provide adequate and appropriate stimulation, or to value and show their belief in their children. The parental support and encouragement children need to overcome the everyday challenges of life may not always be available in violent homes.

# CHAPTER 2

# Links with child abuse and neglect

Parents who are violent towards each other are at increased risk of abusing their children.

> *My dad has also hurt me on occasions. He would throw drinks over me and the[n] kick and punch me in the head but then he would make me stop crying and tell me it didn't hurt. He would tell me it was all my fault and that's why he hit me.*
>
> (Humphreys and Stanley, 2006, p 58)

It should not, however, be assumed that the perpetrator of the domestic violence is responsible for the abuse of the child. Many women who are victims of domestic violence are physically violent towards their children.

There is little agreement on the rates of overlap between

domestic violence and child physical abuse, which range from 45 per cent to 70 per cent. Studies that have explored fatal child abuse perpetrated by fathers have found that, in three-quarters of cases, the man had also been violent towards his partner (Cavanagh *et al*, 2007). Serious case reviews have consistently shown that domestic violence features in approximately half the families where a child is seriously injured or dies.

*He used to say, 'I'm going to kill you at night-time when you are all asleep'. He used to come in with an axe and say 'I am going to kill you'.*
(Mullender *et al*, 2002, p 94)

Child maltreatment, when there is evidence of domestic violence, is not restricted to physical abuse. Simply witnessing or hearing parental distress can have adverse effects on children and could be considered a form of emotional abuse. It is thought that the majority of children living in violent households have been present in the next or same room when the incidents have occurred. For example, practically three-quarters of children who have experienced domestic violence have witnessed the physical assault of their mother and 10 per cent the rape of their mother (McGee, 2000).

There is also evidence that shows that domestic violence is associated with the sexual abuse of children (Humphreys and Stanley, 2006). Fathers and father figures are more likely to sexually abuse the child when they are violent and abusive towards the mother.

## Children's experiences of violence in the home

Children witness, to a greater or lesser extent, every aspect of domestic violence. This can include persistent and brutal violence including killings with knives, ropes and poison.

*He would come in and rip my mother's clothes off. He tried to strangle her, just beat her up like... We were always watching it...*

(NCH Action for Children, 1994, p 31)

Some children will have been forced to be present during the assault. The abuser may have made them watch or encouraged them to be abusive towards their mother. In most cases the child will have been too young, weak or frightened to intervene, which will have left them feeling powerless, angry, responsible and guilty. To witness or hear the violence and see the physical and emotional suffering of their mother is extremely damaging to children.

Many violent men punish their children inappropriately and too harshly. The child may have been threatened with violence or physically hurt in order to frighten and control the mother. Children may also have been physically injured during a violent altercation. They may be the intended victims of an assault as part of a violent incident, injured while trying to stop the violence and protect their abused mother, or be caught inadvertently in the crossfire. Family breakup due to domestic violence does not automatically mean that children are safe from further violence. Abusive men may use contact sessions to emotionally manipulate the children with the aim of punishing the mother.

Some children will have to leave home in an emergency, abandoning everything, including much-loved pets, clothes and toys.

13

The sense of loss will increase when the move to perhaps a refuge or temporary accommodation, such as a bed and breakfast hotel or hostel, results in a change of school and a loss of contact with wider family and friends. Many children fail to understand what is happening and are left feeling bewildered and bereft.

Children can respond in a variety of ways to living with domestic violence. Some will appear to be relatively unscathed, particularly if they have relatives and friends to turn to for support, or if they are less aware of what is going on. Others will recover once they feel safe. Nonetheless, children are likely to be affected by the fear and disruption that they experience and show their distress in different ways depending on their age and developmental stage; no one age group in childhood seems more or less protected from, or damaged by, domestic violence.

## Impact on children's health and development

In order to provide support and care for fostered and adopted children who have experienced domestic violence (and the frequent co-existing problems such as parental substance misuse and poor parental mental health), it is important to understand how the violence may have impacted on children's health and development. Because this differs depending on age, what follows is an exploration of how domestic violence may impact on the unborn child, before turning to focus on children under five, middle year children and finally, adolescents. For each age group, the possible impact of domestic violence is discussed in relation to the child's health, education (including their cognitive and language development), emotional and behavioural development and self-care skills, identity and social presentation, and family and social relationships.

# CHAPTER 3

# The impact on children under five years

## The unborn child

It is not relevant to explore the range of developmental dimensions in relation to the unborn child. The focus, therefore, is on the ways in which domestic violence may impact on the developing foetus.

The unborn child needs nourishment and a safe environment. The child's nutritional needs will be satisfied if the mother has an adequate diet. To ensure that the environment is safe, the mother should refrain from smoking, recreational drugs, unnecessary medication and alcohol. In addition, physical impacts, collisions, bumps and blows, which could damage the placenta and harm the foetus, should be avoided.

The unborn child is therefore not safe from harm when the prospective mother is living in a violent household. In fact, pregnancy can trigger an assault.

*I was in a bad relationship, my partner was battering me black and blue; it started when I was pregnant.*

(Cleaver *et al*, 2007, p 216)

Violence may increase both in its severity and frequency at the time of pregnancy. The assaults may involve beatings, choking, attacks with weapons and sexual assault. The unborn baby is threatened because the incidents frequently include punches or kicks directed at the woman's abdomen. Such violence can, for example, result in miscarriage, stillbirth, premature birth, foetal brain injury, fractures and placental separation.

High levels of maternal stress, evident in mothers experiencing domestic violence, can also result in the unborn baby experiencing higher than expected levels of physical illness, developmental delay, neurological dysfunction and behavioural disturbance. The link may be indirect; high levels of stress may lead the prospective mother to increase her smoking, drug or alcohol intake or turn to prescription drugs for help. The problems may be exacerbated because women experiencing domestic violence often fail to regularly attend antenatal care. This may be due to low self-esteem and depression or to the controlling nature of her abuser.

## Infant development

When fostering or adopting a baby or infant who has grown up in a violent home, an understanding of the underlying issues will help in addressing the young child's needs. The term infant is used here to refer to children from birth to five years.

### Health

Recent research has debunked the assumption that babies and

very young children are unaware of and consequently shielded from the emotional impact of domestic violence (Glaser, 2000). Infancy is potentially the most vulnerable period because it is the time of greatest post-natal brain development. The nature of the baby's day-to-day experiences, including interactions with their parents, determine which brain circuits are reinforced and retained in the baby's brain. When the predominant early experience is fear and stress, the neurochemical responses affect the way the brain develops. Trauma elevates stress hormones, such as cortisol, and high levels of cortisol during infancy increase the brain structure involved in vigilance and arousal. For such infants, the slightest stress unleashes a new surge of stress hormones resulting in, for example, hyperarousal, aggressive responses, hyperactivity, anxiety and impulsive behaviour.

Infants exposed to domestic violence can experience such a state of fear that systems in the brain involved in thinking are shut down. Consequently, all aspects of development, including speech and language, are negatively affected. Although there is little evidence of what happens when the child's circumstances improve, what does exist suggests that many children who are adopted show a remarkable capacity for change and recovery.

The health of babies and young children may be affected through physical injury. For example, the baby or toddler may be in his or her mother's arms when an assault takes place. Domestic violence and its impact on the mother's mental health may also affect her concentration, with dangerous consequences for her infant. Accidents may occur because the mother is less attentive and leaves her young child unsupervised while, for example, sitting in the bath or playing in the home, or she fails to ensure that her child does not leave the house or play on the street unattended.

## Education – cognitive and language development

Infancy is the time of rapid language development. To progress, children need encouragement to extend their language skills, and they need adults to listen to them and help them to take part in conversations. Being read to increases the child's vocabulary, knowledge and understanding of words and language. Children need a safe environment in which they are encouraged to explore and thus develop their cognitive skills.

An infant who has lived in a violent household may show language and cognitive delay. This could have a number of causes. Birth parents who are subject to domestic violence and are experiencing poor mental health may be too preoccupied with their own feelings and emotions to focus on their infants and prioritise their needs.

A lack of self-confidence and self-worth may limit the parent's capacity to engage with the child, to listen to what he or she says and offer praise and encouragement, and to promote learning. The infant's efforts to communicate may be met with indifference and even hostility rather than enjoyment and interest. This can lead to attachment difficulties and other longer-term negative interactions.

The child's cognitive development may also be affected because growing up in a violent and chaotic household can result in children learning to suppress any interest in their surroundings. A pre-school facility like a nursery or playgroup can compensate for a lack of stimulation in the home and offer the child a safe place to learn to play with other children and to interact with adults. Unfortunately, parents who are subjected to domestic violence often fail to take their children on a regular basis. This may be because they are depressed, under the influence of drugs or alcohol, frightened of going out of the home or prevented from attending by their abuser.

## Emotional and behavioural development

*The primary task to be accomplished during the first year of life is for the baby to develop trust in others.*

(Fahlberg, 1994, p 64)

The attachment process begins during the first year of life and continues through infancy. The young child's experience of attachment influences the development of his or her working model of how people are likely to behave towards them. A key factor for its positive development is the presence of a consistent adult who is able to reduce the child's anxiety in stressful situations.

The process of developing secure attachments may be physically interrupted for children living in violent households. For example, the violent parent may be arrested or the abused parent may have to flee the home. As a result, the child may have to experience several unplanned separations, or the loss of a parent figure who fails to return home. Such events can leave them with feelings of extreme anxiety which they express though aberrant behaviours such as rocking, head-banging, disturbed sleep and bed-wetting.

In the very early years, a child's sense of self is wrapped up in their parents' psychological well-being. The baby's emotions and behaviours are to a great extent related to the moods and actions of those who are caring for them. The apathy, despair and sense of worthlessness that many abused parents feel may leave them emotionally unavailable and incapable of showing any warmth towards their children. As a result, the child can become "touch hungry" and unduly clingy because they feel insecure and fearful. If the child has not experienced love and affection, they will feel that they are unloved, rejected and unlovable.

The challenge for many adoptive parents and foster carers is the frequent behavioural and emotional problems that a child who has been exposed to domestic violence exhibits. For example, in addition to the rocking, head-banging, disturbed sleep and bed-wetting, the child may be very fearful, unnaturally quiet, withdrawn or desperate in his or her efforts to please as a result of feeling terror and confusion when witnessing violent assaults on a parent. Such feelings can be compounded when the child perceives their parent as powerless, untrustworthy or rejecting.

## Identity and social presentation

A child's sense of who they are develops during their first five years of life. For example, by the age of three or four, children generally know who their parents and siblings are, and have a sense of who belongs to their immediate family. In violent and chaotic households where apparent family members are transient, this may be confusing. Siblings may live away from home, and there may be a series of occasions when mother and child have to seek refuge with friends or relatives.

At this stage in their development, a child's sense of identity is concrete and based on visible characteristics, such as whether they are a boy or girl, what colour hair they have and the things they are good at doing. This is the period when children are integrating the "good" and "bad" aspects of self through adults telling them how to behave.

Parents who are experiencing domestic violence and who have poor mental health may neglect their own and their children's physical care. As a result, basic hygiene may be ignored and the child left unwashed, with infested hair and dressed in dirty clothes. Although a few children of four years will be able to see to their own needs, younger ones will not, and how they look will influence how they feel about themselves.

Perhaps most damaging to a young child's sense of identity is the belief that they are in some way to blame for the violence in the home and even very young children can try and put things right.

*He smashed my head against the wall because [the baby] was making a mess…I just collapsed on the floor. [The baby] was trying to pull me across the floor crying…saying, 'Mummy, get up'.*
(NCH Action for Children, 1994, p 32)

A very young child may try to look after their distressed mother. For instance, the child may attempt to make her feel better through making a cup of tea, with all the inherent dangers.

Foster carers and adoptive parents can be faced with a child who is struggling to understand who and what they are. They may appear old beyond their years, having assumed too much responsibility while living with their birth family. The lack of guidance may have left them unsure of how to behave and what are acceptable ways of acting, wary of giving voice to their wishes and needs, and uncertain of how adults will respond to them.

### Family and social relationships

The first year of life is the period when children bond with their parents and have an urgent need to be near them. It is the time when the fear of strangers and of separation is at its height. If the relationship with the birth parent is well established, such fears gradually diminish by the time children are three and four years old. These early years are also when children start to establish relationships with other children and learn how to be social beings.

Young children who live in violent households are likely to experience inconsistent parenting, which can be very frightening. The child may never know what will happen and whether their

SECTION 1

needs and wishes will be met with interest and pleasure or with hostility or indifference. As a result, the child may have become fearful and unnaturally vigilant, believing that they are in continual danger. To survive, the child has to learn to suppress all feelings in order to prevent further frightening responses from their parents. The likely outcome will be a child with insecure attachment, who is apathetic and disinterested in his or her environment.

Young children copy the behaviour of their parents. Growing up in a household where violence is commonplace can lead children to assume that aggression is an acceptable way to deal with frustration and get what they want. Children as young as three and four years who have been exposed to domestic violence show more aggression, anger and behaviour problems than non-exposed children. They may have problems in playing and interacting in a sociable way with other children and behave in challenging ways when faced with the needs and wishes of other children in pre-school situations. They will model their parents' behaviour in their relationships with peers, relatives and with their pets.

> *Like my son, he had this thing with hitting little girls; I would just see him hitting on little girls.*
> (DeVoe and Smith, 2002, p 1086)

When looking after babies and very young children who have grown up in violent households, foster carers and adoptive parents will need to offer unconditional love, consistency and a constant presence. Their child will need to feel protected and be reassured that they now live in a safe environment. The child needs to understand that the use of aggression and violence are not acceptable and that there are better and more rewarding ways of dealing with frustration.

# CHAPTER 4

# The impact on middle year children

Middle year children include those aged between five and 12 years. Adopting or fostering a child in this age group will be a greater challenge if they have experienced domestic violence, with all its negative effects, for longer.

## Health

Children who have reached middle childhood and have no speech or hearing problems or a learning disability should have a well-developed vocabulary and communicate easily with adults and children. Although children's co-ordination is improving, they frequently over-estimate their ability and injure themselves during normal play. Only a small proportion of children in middle childhood suffer from any form of mental disorder, although boys (10 per cent) are twice as likely to be affected as girls (five per cent) (Green et al, 2005).

When children live with domestic violence, they continue to be vulnerable as they reach middle childhood; domestic violence is strongly associated with the physical abuse of children. The child may be assaulted by their father (or other man within the household) during a violent outburst, or caught in the crossfire or hurt when trying to intervene between their warring parents. In such situations, physical violence towards children is not the prerogative of men; mothers may also be responsible.

There is clear evidence that a significant group of children who grow up with domestic violence are the victims of child sexual abuse (Humphreys and Stanley, 2006). In the majority of cases, the perpetrator will be the violent father (or mother's partner). In some cases where a birth father is the victim of violence, he will groom his young child for sexual exploitation. The atmosphere of fear within such households will mean that the violated child is very unlikely to reveal what is happening or to seek help.

Research also suggests that children who have grown up with the stress of domestic violence have other, less obviously related, health problems (Onyskiw, 2003). They are found to be at increased risk of sustaining injuries (other than those directly related to the domestic violence), developing allergies and psychosomatic complaints, such as headaches, stomach disorders, nausea, diarrhoea, and sleep disturbances, such as insomnia, nightmares, night terrors and sleepwalking.

The majority of children in this age group enjoy and attend school regularly. Teachers are generally liked and most children have at least one friend. They have an increasing ability to concentrate and are able to screen out distractions and focus on a single issue.

Domestic violence is associated with delays in children's intellectual and cognitive development. This may have been caused during the birth mother's pregnancy when high levels of stress affected the development of the unborn child, but alternatively, the delays may be caused by environmental factors. When starting school, the child living with domestic violence may experience difficulty in concentrating because problems at home dominate their thoughts. Schooling may also be affected because children exposed to domestic violence are more likely to show aggression and to experience difficulty in adhering to school rules.

Educational delays can result when birth parents do not support their children to attend school regularly. School attendance may be erratic because the chaotic lifestyle that frequently accompanies domestic violence often leaves young children having to take care of themselves, including getting to school. Disruptions to the child's education can also be caused by unplanned moves when, for example, mother and child must flee the violence, which then necessitates a change of school.

Growing up with domestic violence does not automatically have a negative impact on a child's learning. For some, school offers a safe haven from their troubled home circumstances. School can be used as an escape where a child can gain a sense of accomplishment through sport, music and drama or academic achievement.

## Emotional and behavioural development and self-care skills

Children of this age are usually happy to confide in known and trusted adults and seek comfort from them when distressed. In most situations, children are then able to manage their emotions when upset, although when very stressed they may revert to more infantile behaviour. If the child is frustrated or angry, boys, in particular, can be verbally aggressive, although physical aggression is less usual.

Living with domestic violence affects children's emotions and behaviour. It can result in children experiencing high levels of anxiety and fear. If adults are seen as untrustworthy and not dependable, the child may exert such rigid control in order to cope that they become emotionally unreachable. Others will have difficulty in controlling outbursts of emotions. They may have violent mood swings oscillating from periods of aggression to periods of extreme passivity. Children may develop a pattern of frequent and violent temper tantrums that they direct at their birth mother, siblings or friends. Some children of this age focus their aggression and violence on animals. Exposure to domestic violence, perpetrated by the father, has been found to be particularly associated with animal cruelty (Currie, 2006).

The ways children react to domestic violence will be influenced by their gender. Although boys and girls may be equally affected by their parents' problems, their responses tend to differ. Boys are more likely to act out their distress with antisocial and aggressive behaviours such as stealing, lying, attention-seeking and attacks on their peers. In contrast, girls tend to respond by internalising their worries, showing symptoms of depression, anxiety and withdrawal. Gender is not always linked to the way emotional distress is exhibited; girls can also be aggressive and violent while some boys will be withdrawn and depressed.

The child's temperament is also a factor. Some children may have learnt to cope with the stress of domestic violence, including the unpredictable, unexpected and irrational behaviour of their parents, by seeking to escape. One possible method of escape is to develop a fantasy world where the frightening behaviour of their parents is interpreted in acceptable ways. Although effective in violent circumstances, it can result in later difficulties if it becomes the child's established way of dealing with stress. Other children will learn to cope by withdrawing into themselves, while for some, fear for their own safety will have taught them to seek a place of physical safety.

> *I thought that he was going to hit me too...I ran into the other room and shut the door.*

(Joseph *et al*, 2006, p 34)

The strategies children devise to protect themselves will inevitably shape their future response to stress. The child quoted above may have to create his own safe space wherever he goes; the child who retreats into a fantasy world could be in danger of permanently living in it.

## Identity and social presentation

This is the age when children develop a more global sense of who they are. Their experience of family and peers will result in an evaluation of their self-worth on which the child's self-esteem is built.

There is evidence to suggest that being of the same gender as the adult perpetrating the violence negatively affects the child's self-esteem and appears to be more traumatic and disturbing than for a child of the opposite sex (Fantuzzo and Lindquist, 1989).

The existing relationship between the child and the abuser is also pertinent to the impact of domestic violence. Children are likely to be more affected when the violence is perpetrated by their biological father or their stepfather rather than by a recent substitute parent figure. Children who have seen their own father abuse their mother may be particularly traumatised. Seeing their parents unable to control themselves or their circumstances may leave the child feeling helpless, as well as confused and uncertain about their own identity.

27

The wish to protect and look after a parent, even at this young age, may result in the child assuming responsibilities that are normally beyond their years. For example, calling the emergency services for the police or an ambulance may become a part of everyday life.

> *Sam [nine years] took responsibility for protecting their mother from assaults by telephoning the police from a public callbox, or by shouting until the neighbours came to help.*
> (Brandon and Lewis, 1996, p 39)

The failure to prevent or stop their parents' violence may leave some children feeling guilty and inadequate, or they may come to believe, or be told, that their behaviour triggers the violent outbursts. If they are taught that the problems lie with themselves rather than their parents, then their sense of self-worth will be seriously diminished.

## Family and social relationships

Children in middle childhood enjoy physical closeness and generally have a confiding relationship with a parent. They may find discussing their feelings difficult and prefer to talk about them after the event.

Living with domestic violence may affect the child's ability to form rewarding relationships. For example, domestic violence may cause the birth parents to behave in inconsistent and unexpected ways, which children of this age would find difficult to understand. The child may become fearful and learn to anticipate hostility because domestic violence can mean that commonplace aspects of life are subjected to a frightening and pervasive control.

28

The relationship between the child and his or her parents may be undermined if the child's expectations of parental care and protection are not met. The child may be left feeling betrayed, let down and angry. Alternatively, the feelings of betrayal may be the result of having been forced, by the male perpetrator, to witness their mother's abuse – emotional, physical and sexual.

> *I was mad with my daddy for hurting my mummy and me and my sisters and brother…*
>
> (Barron, 2007, p 14)

If the child has seen his or her mother sexually assaulted and humiliated, it will debase their relationship, not to mention the negative impact on the child's perception of the father or father figure.

Many children will become adept at caring for the parent who is subject to assaults or at mediating between fighting parents. Such a highly developed sense of responsibility can have a knock-on effect on other aspects of their childhood like school attendance and peer friendships.

Friendships with peers are of growing importance to children in their middle years. Friends and opportunities to play outside the home may provide the child with an escape from the pressures of their family life.

> *I wouldn't say anything [about the domestic violence], but when we're playing I forget all of this [the abuse] for a while.*
>
> (Joseph et al, 2006, p 32)

But not all children have this opportunity for friendships. Growing

SECTION 1

up with domestic violence can restrict relationships with peers. Children may be reluctant to have friends visit the home, or bringing friends home may be discouraged or even forbidden. Learning how to interact with their peers, how to interpret body language and other subtle cues may not be possible for children living with domestic violence. As a result, a child may have few if any friends and suffer peer rejection. Bullying in response to such a situation is not uncommon and can be a consequence of an impaired ability to handle frustration and regulate emotions. The child may have failed to learn effective problem-solving skills and strategies for resolving conflicts without resorting to aggression.

Children rarely talk to anyone about domestic violence and the circumstances in which they are living. Such secrecy can result from a number of factors. Parents may have instilled the need for silence through fear of retribution or possible separation. The child may keep quiet because they recognise the social stigma attached to domestic violence and fear the ridicule of friends, or because they fear no one will believe them. Boys in particular find it hard to talk about emotional issues.

# CHAPTER 5

# The impact on adolescence

## Health

Early adolescence is a period of change and experimentation. Teenagers need reassurance to help them accept the changes to their bodies because these can be confusing and distressing. Some will embark on their first sexual encounter and need advice and accurate factual knowledge about puberty, sex and contraception. The teenage years are also the time when some youngsters experiment with smoking, drinking and drug-taking. To help protect the child, parents and carers need to put in place firm boundaries while providing love, advice, guidance and understanding.

The general health of adolescents living with domestic violence may be neglected. The emotional unavailability that can accompany the violence and the subsequent substance misuse or poor mental health of the birth parent may mean that they are unaware of, and unable to attend to, the child's worries about their changing bodies. Teenagers who feel unloved and unlovable are vulnerable to sexual exploitation, which they can misinterpret as a caring relationship. The exploitation and attendant sexual health problems may be missed if the parents are so absorbed in their own problems that they fail to ensure that children attend routine medical appointments.

The likelihood that children will be physically injured while living in a household where there is domestic violence continues into the teenage years. Teenagers will have learnt to live with the constant fear of violent arguments, threats or actual bodily assault either on themselves or directed at a parent or sibling. If the assailant has a pattern of drink and violence, the risk of assault increases.

*Mum works at night. Dad comes home drunk and beats me up. I dread the nights.*
(ChildLine, 1997, p 31)

In cases where teenagers are not specifically targeted, they may still sustain injuries through attempts to protect one parent from the other.

## Education and cognitive ability

The majority of children attend school regularly during their teenage years. This is encouraged when parents support the child's learning and recognise the importance of school. Education can also take place outside school and with parental support many teenagers are involved in activities such as football, swimming, music or drama.

Domestic violence can seriously affect teenagers' education and learning. Birth parents may not support or encourage the child's learning at home and fail to attend meetings or other school events. Such a lack of involvement with the child's education could be due to the abuser forbidding contact with the school, the victimised parent being frightened of outside scrutiny, or because of self-absorption and apathy on the part of both birth parents.

As for younger children, school can sometimes provide a sanctuary and be a source of help. It may be the one area of their lives which the adolescent feels is "normal". But for many, school life will not be easy. Constant worries over vulnerable family members may make concentration too difficult. On occasions, lessons may be missed because young people feel impelled to stay at home to protect younger siblings or the victimised parent. In addition, teenagers may not have learnt the accepted social skills of interaction with adults outside the home. Domestic violence demonstrates to children that violence is the way to deal with problems, and may lead the adolescent to use violent or aggressive language and behaviour, not only towards pupils but also teachers. An inability to interact successfully with teachers may result in learning deficits and feelings of alienation.

Finally, domestic violence may mean that families have had to move to a new neighbourhood, perhaps more than once, with the inevitable change of schools, interruptions to the teenagers' learning and course work, and a loss of friends, familiar teachers and community.

## Emotional and behavioural development and self-care skills

Adolescence is a time when children strive for independence. But the road is never smooth and there will be times when children need much parental support and reassurance. In early adolescence, emotions are frequently unstable and poorly controlled, which

33

can cause considerable strife with parents. The majority of adolescents' worries centre on school and exams as well as social concerns regarding friends, clothes and general appearance.

The volatility of the teenage years means that the impact of domestic violence becomes more intense. Adolescents may experience extreme feelings of fear, sadness, worthlessness, isolation, depression and thoughts of suicide.

> *I would feel like killing myself because I would think it's my fault, 'cos he drilled it in my head.*
>
> (Humphreys and Stanley, 2006, p 59)

Or they may react differently, with anger, aggression, controlling behaviour and defiance. As discussed in relation to children in their middle years, the behavioural response to such feelings is somewhat related to gender. Girls are more likely to turn their feelings of anger onto themselves, while boys tend to express anger outwardly. Although gender has some impact on how emotions are manifested, no behaviour pattern is specific to boys or girls. Moreover, the child's behaviour may vary over time and include opposite behaviours at different times. The adolescent's personality will also have an impact on their response; siblings in the same family, living through the same events, can react very differently.

> *In one household with three sons the eldest physically fought his father, the youngest became withdrawn, while the middle boy took to staying in his room and developed mental health problems.*
>
> (Humphreys and Stanley, 2006, p 60)

If adolescents see bullying both at school and home as an effective way of solving problems, they may come to believe that it is an acceptable part of family and social relationships, a way to gain control over others, and a justified way to resolve conflicts. As mentioned in relation to younger children, exposure to domestic violence is a strong predictor of children's cruelty to animals. It is of particular concern when it continues into adolescence because teenagers who abuse animals almost always engage in other antisocial behaviours, such as substance abuse. In addition to bullying and animal cruelty, domestic violence is also associated with an increased likelihood of adolescent boys indulging in sexually abusive behaviour.

Children's aberrant behaviour is frequently a cry for help, a wish for adults to recognise their difficulties and to help them to sort things out.

## Identity and social presentation

Parents and close relatives act as role models for children and their beliefs and values are passed from one generation to the next. Adolescence, however, is the time for questioning, but the rigid thinking that is often a product of domestic violence may lead to wholesale rejection of parental values. Without anything to replace them, this can undermine an already uncertain sense of identity.

The lifestyle of some teenagers who have experienced domestic violence would suggest that it has left them with a poor self-image and very low self-esteem. Adolescents are acutely aware of the stigma associated with neglect because they are conscious of their appearance and sensitive to how others see them. If family income is spent on alcohol or drugs or is tightly controlled by the aggressive and violent parent, teenagers can find it difficult to keep up an acceptable appearance, which may lead to teasing and compound feelings of low self-worth.

Adolescents who grow up in violent households are forced to assume too much responsibility for themselves and other family members. They feel responsible for protecting younger siblings and their vulnerable parent from both emotional violence and physical assault. Such a feeling of overall responsibility and fear of what might happen can result in some teenagers being in a state of constant vigilance. The tendency to blame themselves for their parents' violent behaviour will leave them with feelings of guilt, inadequacy and powerlessness.

## Family and social relationships

The teenage years are a period when children slowly gain autonomy. The process is generally turbulent and takes time to accomplish. Young people need a caring parent who understands them, offers unqualified love, and allows them to retreat into childhood when necessary.

Domestic violence can affect every aspect of family and social relationships. Simply witnessing the violence can have devastating consequences for a child's relationship with their birth parents. In most cases adolescents abhor the violence. Some will be overwhelmed with feelings of anger, which they direct at both abuser and abused, towards the abuser for the violence and towards the abused for accepting the behaviour. Emotions are complex, for although children may feel angry and let down by their parents, they usually continue to love them, leaving themselves with ambivalent and conflicting feelings.

Domestic violence also affects teenagers' friendships. The unreliability of parental behaviour may make adolescents cautious of exposing their family to outside scrutiny. When bringing friends home is impossible and friendships have to be restricted or curtailed, adolescents become very isolated. Teenagers may also avoid close friendships because they wish to keep information about their family secret. Such secrecy may be a self-imposed decision or the result of parental cajolement and/or threats.

*He says that if we ever tell anyone he will kill us.*
(ChildLine, 1997, p 23)

Some teenagers may be fortunate to have friends and relatives in whom they can confide and who provide important support and role models. Mutual peer friendships, if they can be achieved and maintained, are associated with feelings of self-worth and can protect adolescents from some of the negative consequences of growing up with domestic violence.

One method young people may use to cope with the stress of living with domestic violence is distancing themselves from their birth parents and home. For example, a teenager may learn to withdraw emotionally through music, reading, video games, online virtual worlds or watching TV. For others, withdrawal may be physical through staying in their room, spending much of their time away from home or running away.

Although withdrawal, either emotional and/or physical, may help teenagers to avoid the danger and stress of domestic violence, it can become an established way of dealing with all emotional and stressful situations. Such an approach can be destructive for all relationships and can continue into adulthood.

CHAPTER **6**

# The challenge facing adoptive parents and foster carers

Having explored in some detail the impact of domestic violence on children of different ages, this section summarises the challenges that adoptive or foster families face.

## Babies and young children

Exposure to domestic violence has a demonstrable effect even on very young children. Infants and young children may be given to incessant crying, rocking, head-banging, screaming and have poor sleep patterns. When these behaviours occur, the child can be difficult to comfort. There are a number of possible causes for such behaviours, including neurological damage sustained while intra-uterine, fear of violence, actual parental violence and neglect, or childhood accidents due to poor parental supervision.

The young child may show little or no emotional affect, reflecting a history of insecure attachment due to frequent, unplanned separations, lack of parental warmth, love and affection. There may be frequent outbursts of inappropriate and aggressive behaviours that have resulted from modelling parental violence.

Young children may also display delayed cognitive and language development. This could be the result of brain damage arising from physical abuse and neglect, or from a lack of stimulation, parental interest and encouragement.

Many children will catch up rapidly on language and cognitive deficits when provided with a safe, supportive and loving environment. Similarly, the majority of babies and toddlers will moderate their behaviours and emotional responses when they are offered consistent emotional warmth and loving attention. To develop the most expedient approach, new parents should work closely with relevant professionals, such as nursery or playgroup staff, as well as health visitors and doctors. When little or no progress is observed, professional expertise should be sought in order to explore possible neurological damage.

## Middle childhood

The experience of domestic violence in middle childhood can cause a number of health issues including allergies, psychosomatic complaints and sleep problems. A history of physical abuse or sexual assault can leave children afraid of physical contact or prone to displaying inappropriate sexual behaviour. Children may show cognitive delay because living with domestic violence has affected their ability to concentrate, or disrupted their schooling.

Children's emotional and behavioural development can be the cause of considerable concern. The experience of violence may have left children withdrawn and difficult to reach, while others are unduly attention seeking and have problems controlling their temper, display aggression, and behave in an antisocial manner.

When children feel to some degree responsible for the violence within their birth family, they are frequently left with low self-esteem and feelings of helplessness and guilt.

Many children will have difficulty forming relationships with adults. A history of inconsistent and frightening parenting, inappropriate parental control, and witnessing violence may have left children distrustful of all adults, regardless of how well meaning they may be. Peer relationships may also be difficult because children have not learnt to control their frustrations or develop effective inter-personal skills.

Children in middle childhood will pose a greater challenge than younger children because they have probably experienced domestic violence for longer and behaviour patterns have become more established. To catch up with any educational delays and encourage learning, new parents need to raise children's self-esteem and self-belief. For some children, this will entail working closely with schools to develop an appropriate work programme.

There are no short cuts when tackling well-established emotional and behavioural responses. Essential to the child's sense of security and self-esteem will be the knowledge that their new parents will love and support them when things go wrong. For some children, love may not be enough and psychological help is needed. Expert advice should always be sought when children display inappropriate sexual behaviour or cruelty to younger children and animals.

## Adolescents

Teenagers may be involved in inappropriate sexual activity as a result of experiencing domestic violence. Feelings of worthlessness can lead them to seek comfort and self-realisation in early and unsafe sexual relationships. This pattern of behaviour can be difficult to alter because it reflects the young person's low self-esteem and lack of self-respect.

Adolescence is a period of emotional turmoil. The experiences of growing up with domestic violence increase the turbulence of emotions and the ability to control behavioural responses. Gender influences how emotions are dealt with. Girls are more likely to turn their anger and fear inwards resulting in, for example, self-harm and eating disorders. Boys tend to express their anger through aggression and anti-social behaviours. Some youngsters feel so threatened by strong emotions and stress that they withdraw emotionally or physically. Running away from home is one aspect of withdrawal that can place children in very dangerous situations.

For all young people the teenage years are a period of experimentation and exploration and key to influencing their behaviour is the development of a relationship of trust. More than anything else, teenagers need to know that somebody whom they trust cares about them, is interested in what they do, and will forgive them for minor transgressions. Trust and respect, however, take time to establish and to build such a relationship with adolescents who have experienced a lifetime of rejection and disappointment is not an easy task.

To develop a relationship that allows the discussion of emotions and problems is particularly important and will enable adoptive parents to build up a young person's self-esteem and self-respect, qualities that are essential for ensuring safe and appropriate

SECTION I

sexual relationships. For example, young people need to develop the necessary coping strategies to act effectively and to acquire sufficient self-confidence to influence what happens to them.

For some youngsters, a stable environment and a trusting and supportive relationship may not be enough and professional psychological or psychiatric help should be sought. A strong indication that professional intervention is needed is when teenagers are violent or sexually abusive or cruel towards animals. Animal cruelty is often linked to high levels of interpersonal violence and is likely to be a symptom of deep psychological problems. If such issues remain unresolved, they herald violence in adulthood including criminal violence for both males and females.

## Conclusion

*There is no excuse for giving up on the grounds that the child is too old for anything to make any difference.*
(Rutter, 1985, p 395)

Children's powers of recovery are considerable despite the difficulties and uncertainties they have experienced through living with domestic violence. It is never too late to intervene, as the two stories that follow richly illustrate.

# PARENTING CHILDREN AFFECTED BY DOMESTIC VIOLENCE

HELEN DUNNING

MELINDA RIGOPOULO

# Can we break the cycle?

**Helen Dunning**

**Making decisions**

I came to consider adoption as a means of building my family in the winter of 2001. I was a single woman whose long-term relationship had broken down two years before and, at the age of 32, I was reviewing my options. I had a relative who was a single adoptive parent and so I knew it was possible to adopt as a single woman. When I considered what was most important, and with some strong female role models who were single parents, I decided that if I missed out on being a mother I would always regret it. I didn't tell many people of my plans until I had been approved but the family members I told, to sound out their views, were supportive, and so with their backing the journey began.

**Starting the journey**

I started the process just after Christmas of 2001. It was fairly straightforward, I got on well with my very experienced social worker, and I enjoyed reflecting on my life so far and looking forward to the future. My childhood wasn't perfect; although my parents were professional people, our family had its issues with a stressed and dominating father, struggling with the legacy of his own childhood, and a mother who immersed herself in work to make herself feel needed.

The adoption assessment was thorough; I filled in my initial application form and had a meeting with the social worker to discuss proceeding. I was worried my weight would be held against me but I could prove I was fit and active; even so, my medical was done early to put my mind at rest.

I was invited to join a preparation group: three days of learning about children who need families with homework between sessions. It felt like being on show where everything I said (and didn't) would be analysed to see if I was "fit" to look after a vulnerable child.

The hardest part of the process for me was looking at why children come into the care system and the resulting behavioural and emotional problems. Although we may "know" why it happens, it is something else to be looking at children's profiles knowing that one day you could be parenting a child who has had some of those experiences.

After the preparation group came the home study, even more thorough, with information required about my attitudes and behaviours, finances, childhood, family background, hobbies, references, where a child would fit into my life, and more. I used to joke that my social worker knew what colour knickers I wore every day because she knew everything else about me.

After our fortnightly meetings ended, I was approved at panel to adopt one child between the ages of four and seven. My social worker and I then started to look at children's profiles and Child Permanence Reports (CPRs) to find the child who would eventually become a part of my family. As I was looking for a child between the ages of four and seven (as a single woman I knew I would have to return to work eventually), it didn't take long to find a little boy of six who needed a new mummy. He was near the top of my age range and had been overlooked by many adopters due to his lack of speech, but that didn't put me off. What really drew me to Lee was the vulnerability of the child I saw in the video. He had been diagnosed with global developmental delay and had a Statement of Special Educational Needs at school. He was described as having a speech and language delay due to neglect; he hadn't been spoken to at home and was not taken to Speech and Language Therapy (SALT) when referred by the health visitor. In fact, he had no speech at all when he came into care, just grunts and noises, but his foster carers made me a video, so I could get used to the pattern of the sounds he made.

It was the fact that he was removed due to domestic violence (including threats against his and his siblings' lives) that made me feel I could offer this little boy a safe future with lots of love and support to reach his full potential. The chronology of Lee's life revealed that although a serious incident led to his final removal, there was also a catalogue of five years of incidents; each time the family had been given "another chance" in an effort to keep them together. These five years have probably caused the most damage, and I see it in my son's behaviour most days.

My whole family has been touched by domestic violence for at least three generations, so I knew how important it was to break the cycle for him; I'm aware of the impact it can have on families and child witnesses who often recreate their experiences in their future relationships. It was also obvious to me that I would understand some of Lee's difficulties and why he would behave as he did because I recognised that some of my own anxieties and feelings were due to the violence I had witnessed or experienced. After years of counselling I understood myself and hoped that I could help him to do the same.

**Bringing Lee home**

Introductions began with excitement and also the fear of heading into the unknown. What if Lee didn't like me? What if I couldn't manage him? How would I entertain him all day? What about his speech delay?

Introductions lasted six days and Lee gradually transferred from his foster carers to my home, although he was ready and packed the first day I turned up, and couldn't understand why he couldn't just come home with Mummy. He would take my car keys so I couldn't leave without him and always made sure the packed car had the front passenger seat free for him to jump into his little blue booster seat.

His speech was still very unclear but a summer of running around with other children chattering away to him in his foster home had helped, and so it didn't take me long to clue in to his speech pattern, although he was still sometimes difficult to understand.

I drove home the wrong way every day after spending time with Lee and just kept driving as I was too tired to turn around. I used to look for a signpost to a town nearest my own and carry on driving. I really don't remember much about those days as they passed in a fog, but I do remember the harvest festival where I was introduced to everyone as Lee's "new mummy", and also the first time I had to take him back to his foster home in his pyjamas after a full day with me, including teatime and bath time. It was a real wrench to leave him that evening knowing he was crying for me when I put him to bed. I eventually set off home at two in the morning when I knew he was settled and asleep. I hadn't realised how upset I would feel leaving him behind when he was distressed, but I also felt really inadequate as I had no idea at that point how to settle him, and was reliant on his foster carers to help me out.

After six days it was time to bring Lee home permanently, and although it felt great I was terrified! He was excited and couldn't wait to get moving. This was when I really started to get to know him; it was a time of sheer exhaustion and huge excitement. I also quickly managed to pick up on Lee's speech and with the help of some tips from a speech and language therapist friend, we would chat away for hours. Lee managed to have a way of describing something that I could just about understand, and this made me feel sure I'd made the right decision in choosing him. He was a whirling dervish, constantly on the move, looking at the next thing to do and he wouldn't be left alone for a second of the day.

Friends with daughters asked if he had ADHD whilst friends with sons said he was a typical boy, which made me think that everything would be OK.

Somehow I managed to get things done with a six-year-old perched on either my knee or my hip. He was terrified to be left on his own in a room and needed to be with me constantly. Don't ever laugh when adoptive parents tell you they cheer the first time they get to go to the bathroom on their own, they're not kidding!

Lee was also very controlling. I was once refused petrol because he wouldn't let go of the pump and get back in the car, and cooking his tea was a nightmare. The best strategy was to cook when he was at school and just reheat it in the microwave when he was ready. He couldn't wait for food; he would try to take cold food out of the oven telling me it was ready to eat. It was impossible to limit his food as the years of neglect made him constantly fear hunger, so the answer was to have a lunchbox in the fridge full of healthy snacks he could help himself to during the day to supplement his breakfast, dinner, tea and supper. It also helped to take it when visiting friends' houses, as he would pronounce he was hungry and ask for food as soon as he entered the front door.

The sheer terror of Lee's early experiences became most apparent at bedtime. Being tucked in after a story and then kissed goodnight would unleash either manic behaviour or screaming at the top of the stairs. Any little noise outside would immediately send him into a panic. The owls were not his friends! I quickly discovered that to stay with him until he fell asleep would result in a better evening routine even though I was exhausted and

SECTION II

needed a cup of tea. For the first five years I would wake at every little noise, so when Lee had night terrors, I could be there for him, and I found that the best strategy was to lift him out of bed and gently soothe him; he couldn't tell me what was wrong so I gave up asking and concentrated on settling him back to sleep.

Yet these were also the loveliest times we had. Lee's speech and language delay meant that making big gestures and facial expressions became a part of life, so there was fun in whatever we did with lots of laughter. He was so lovely and cuddly and we'd snuggle up on the sofa to watch cartoons together or play hide and seek whilst waiting for his bath to run. But he always hid in the same place!

## Primary school blues

Lee got through primary school fairly unscathed, although I found it frustrating that the teachers and his support workers didn't understand some of his behaviours; they expected him to lie on the floor during PE with his eyes closed to relax and to walk into a loud and busy classroom, not understanding that he needed to be in there first to scan for danger. Lining up was another problem as he would feel threatened by other pupils standing behind him, and couldn't cope with the jostling and pushing.

The teachers were desperate to diagnose him, but needed my signature to allow any professional to observe Lee. I refused because a diagnosis wouldn't result in any further support and could hinder his future prospects, when what he really needed was to settle into family life and be my son. I did a lot of research about the different diagnoses they were talking about and discovered that they all have overlapping symptoms, so we could have ended up with a range of diagnoses depending on who saw him. He did have some speech and language input but struggled in the group as he always wanted to answer and became frustrated when he wasn't understood. In individual therapy I was told that I was doing everything that could be done by repeating what he was trying to say without pushing him or expecting him to repeat it correctly.

I decided to parent therapeutically instead of attempting to find answers, by trying to understand what he needed, by not using punishment but warm and loving consequences that were linked to the problem. So if he was playing outside and falling out with the other children, I would bring him in for a few minutes to stay with me and calm him down before going back out with Mummy watching to make sure he was OK.

The school staff also managed to make me feel inadequate. As if being a new mum wasn't hard enough, I found myself at loggerheads with them weekly over his timetable, and at annual reviews and parents' evenings. He wasn't making progress as fast as they would have liked, and they couldn't understand my frustration at their refusal to see the impact of neglect and domestic violence on his learning. They once told me that we needed to 'separate his learning from his experiences', which many damaged children find impossible to do.

The curriculum was also difficult: baby photos were asked for (which we didn't have), and there was little understanding of the feelings of a small boy who didn't need to be reminded what abuse was by the NSPCC at school assembly.

The school run was hard. Lee wouldn't want to go into class in the morning but tearing him away from the playground at the end of the school day was even harder. I soon worked out it was transitions that he didn't cope with very well and so I made sure we always had time for a little play on the swings to distract from the imminent tantrum that threatened.

Playing in the school yard after school made him realise that not everyone went home at 3.15 and pretty soon he wanted to stay to go to after school club. As I was doing a phased return to work, I was relieved that he was so keen to stay and play, especially when it was discovered that our new boss, due to start in September, didn't like part-time staff and felt maternity leave was "a pain in the neck". It wasn't any easier to pick Lee up after school club though, and by then he was tired and hungry as well, so a little bar of chocolate usually did the trick to prevent the tantrum.

**Hard work at home**

Whilst school was hard, at least it provided some structure to our day and without structure the day could be difficult. I think I only began to relax in school holidays, about four years in, when we had at last found a sort of routine that worked for us.

I always made sure that for some part of the weekend an activity club was on offer and over the years he tried sea scouts, horse riding, skiing, canoeing, windsurfing, water skiing and anything else that would get us out in the fresh air and work off some of the endless energy he seemed to have. All of the activities had one thing in common: Lee needed me there to look out for him and explain his difficulties when things got tricky.

SECTION 11

53

He finally has settled on sailing and seems to enjoy being out in a small boat on his own with no one to tell him what to do. This has built his confidence and has also given him a pathway to follow, as he wants to pursue it as a career after completing his work experience in a supportive placement where he sails weekly.

Unstructured weekend time or trying to get out visiting friends or family was another matter! Any thought of a new place or new thing was met with wild behaviour and running around the house yelling and giggling; anything to get mummy to shout with exasperation 'Right! We're not going', which never in fact happened. I realised Lee was terrified of new experiences as he didn't know what was going to happen, so we agreed we would just try new things for a few minutes and then leave if we needed to, although when he realised what fun he could have, we never did.

I always felt it was important to try new things as otherwise we would be stuck in the house like hermits and he needed to be building his confidence with new situations and new experiences with Mummy there to help him.

I continued with the therapeutic parenting too. No sending Lee to the "naughty step" in our house as he needed to be near me and helped with his behaviour rather than be punished for things he couldn't help due to his earlier experiences and his frustration regarding his lack of speech and my occasional lack of understanding. He needed lots of explanations about things that he just didn't know or comprehend, and we've spent many hours talking and trying to talk.

SECTION II

**Secondary school**

I was starting to look forward to secondary school, as Lee had got into the school I knew could best meet his needs (really the *only* one that could meet his needs) and where I knew I would be welcomed to support and guide the staff to make it the best experience I could for him.

By the time Lee reached secondary school age, I was much more aware of his difficulties and how they could be overcome. The first hurdle would be feeling overwhelmed and scared in a huge school with lots of bigger pupils. Call it fate, but a teaching post came up in this school; I had the right qualifications and experience and I was appointed just before Lee started in Year 7.

Working in Lee's school meant that I could take him in with me before he started – it was like a prolonged introduction period – and knowing Mummy was there to look after him has been of huge benefit to him when things got tough. It also meant that his teachers, my colleagues, were more willing to help and listen, and between us we devised strategies to support him, such as leaving the classroom early to avoid the crush in the corridors, and going to lunch a few minutes before his classmates (the kitchen running out of food and missing his lunch was a massive worry for him). He has needed a lot of support in lessons and social time to cope with the jostling and teasing that is part of secondary school life; he doesn't always understand teasing, and sees it as bullying, which can unleash his anger. Although his speech was much improved by this point, it didn't take long for his peers to realise they could mimic him and get him into trouble.

Again, Lee wasn't making progress as quickly as was expected of him, but a fabulous school and an understanding SENCO (Special Educational Needs Co-ordinator) are your best friends in such a situation. Lee received extra teaching in literacy and numeracy and had one-to-one support in lessons, not only to help him learn but also to act as a buffer between him and the rest of the class, who quickly learnt that teasing him would light a touch paper and get him removed to isolation. I always insisted that he wasn't left in isolation alone but had a support worker with him; in a lot of ways this made learning easier for him and less stressful, as he was then free from distractions and the fear of what was going on at the back of the class that could hurt him.

This constant fear of danger was difficult for school to understand. The boy who was throwing the rugby ball in the air (he's going to throw it at me), the boy fiddling with the machinery in technology (he's trying to cut my hand off), the knives in cooking (he's going to stab me) and the constant insults focused on his weight, his learning needs and the fact that his mum was a teacher and "wouldn't let him do that" – whatever it was he wanted to do, were all perceived as physical and emotional threats of violence.

When things got really tough for him, he would turn up at my classroom door, angry and swearing and complaining about what a bad mum I was for not sorting something out for him. Luckily the staff understood, and the strategy was that whoever was supporting him would know he was heading to me and would follow to take him somewhere to cool down, and I would check later that he was OK.

Choosing GCSE options was fun! We went for options with few exams and subjects that would help his social and independence skills, so ended up with media (understanding the world), film studies (understanding people), graphics (fine motor skills) and the obligatory maths and English. He dropped out of non-qualification subjects to have more time to do his coursework.

Lee did well and obtained some Level 1 GCSE qualifications, which enabled him to say in sixth form; he wasn't ready for college – yet. He has made good progress, considering his poor start in life. I cried when he got a GCSE grade E for English as I never imagined he could do so well. This will help him to get where he needs to be in the future as he can build on his grade to achieve the "magical C" that the Government considers he needs to succeed in life. If only that were all he needed.

Lee was also lucky to be in a supportive and understanding school that recognised that it was better to speak to me rather than to go straight down the safeguarding route, otherwise I could have been the victim of many investigations. In his controlled assessment for his English GCSE, he wrote that he hated his mum because of the awful things she did to him and he wanted to kill himself. The teacher who marked it luckily went to the SENCO who knew of the difficulties we were having, and so spoke to me rather than sending it off to an external moderator who might have reported me to Social Services. On other occasions, Lee would tell staff about something that had happened in his birth family that he couldn't put in a time and place due to his language difficulties, so it could have been mistaken for something that had happened at the

57

weekend rather than years ago.

That doesn't mean it's been easy, for although they were my colleagues, in some ways I felt that I could be blamed for Lee's behaviour.

**Our life away from education**

Lee's relationship with our wider family has always been difficult due to his grief at losing his younger siblings. Although we see them regularly, it's not the same for him and he often feels angry that I have my "birth" family around me, particularly my brother whom we see often. He has a lovely and very positive relationship with my uncle and my step-dad, mimicking the good relationship he had with his birth dad and then his male foster carer.

Lee always had a good relationship with his birth dad. Although he was one of the perpetrators of domestic violence, he was good with his children. He seemed to use violence as a coping mechanism for the mental health issues of Lee's birth mum. I think his birth mum's borderline personality disorder is the reason that Lee is mistrustful of women; I often think I am lucky to have such a good relationship with him, but if I had a male partner, I suspect I would be left to do the chores whilst they would be having all the fun. He always made a beeline for male relatives who would play rough with him and would spend hours doing what he wanted: letting him pretend to drive their cars or playing with his Hornby train set together.

My mother lives far away, but we've had many happy holidays with her in the south of England where we could swim in the sea, play on the beach and go for bike rides in the sun. My mum was always happy to look after us and would happily allow me to sit back and recharge my batteries and leaves me to take care of Lee. New parents are often recommended to do "funnelling": providing everything for their child until the child feels safe and can trust that they now have someone to meet their needs.

As Lee got older, we ventured further afield and now we can confidently take holidays abroad or in this country with friends, when we often holiday together in separate caravans.

## Where are we now?

Luckily, Lee's secondary school offers a one-year course at a level he can manage: a general course to teach him key skills and independence in a small group of students with similar needs, so that he is finally able to make some friends. This year is really working out well for him, he has friends, and he's becoming more independent and enjoying the kudos he gets from being a sixth former. He also benefits from having fewer lessons, more free time and from me not looking over his shoulder every two minutes to see what he's doing and who with.

That's not to say Lee doesn't still need a lot of support – he does. Although now it's more about helping him to make the right choices and making sure he has the backup he needs when things go wrong, as they inevitably do. The things going wrong can be minor, like falling out with a friend or not understanding why his friend is busy, and no, you haven't done anything wrong or upset him. Or something major may happen, like not watching where he's going on his motorbike and hitting the car in front, so that Mum needs to drive up to help him sort out his insurance. It was always Lee's

SECTION II

59

dream to have a motorbike as soon as he could, just like Granddad, my father. But motorbikes can be dangerous and the thought of him at 16 on the road filled me with fear. So I did what we've always done: scaffolded his learning so that he built up what he needed to know slowly, in order to lessen the chance of him forgetting one of the steps and getting it wrong.

So scaffolding goes like this:

- He wants a motorbike at 16.

- At seven he learns to ride a pushbike and when he's confident we take him on quiet roads to ride with me and Granddad (him in the middle) to teach him the rules of the road. He also goes out riding pillion with Granddad on his motorbike as often as possible.

- At 11 I find a local authority youth club that teaches him to maintain and fix motorbikes and to ride safely off road. He does this until he is 15.

- At about 13 he is confident on a motorbike and is also confident on busy roads riding alongside Granddad on his mountain bike.

- At 15 he gets the highway code on his games console to practice hazard perception and plays this as much as he can because he enjoys it.

- At 16 he takes his Compulsory Bike Test (CBT) and is pronounced a "safe rider" and "one of the best I've seen" by the instructor.

- Now he can use his money that we've saved for him since he was six (and we realised how expensive motorbikes are) to buy his first motorbike.

- So at 16 Lee is relatively independent, building his confidence, proud of his progress and ready to look at the future.

**What was hard**

Lee's anger has been the hardest thing to deal with. Anger at his past and the birth parents who let him down so badly that he had to be removed for his own safety. That anger has always been directed at me, his mum who wasn't there in the past but will always love him whatever verbal abuse he throws at me. That to me is the most important thing he needs to know – that I love him enough to forgive him but also to help him so that his rages decrease and he can better verbalise his distress in the future.

It's hard to stand and listen to how useless I am, how stupid, how much he hates me, how I should put him back in care because I don't love him and how he's leaving at 16 to live on his own. His speech has improved enough for him to swear at me clearly and in context when he is angry with me and the world, although I know the person he is really angry with is his birth mother.

It's especially hard knowing that if he was a man I would have thrown him out by now, as my paternal grandma and my mum both threw out their abusive husbands, and as I have in the past thrown out my abusive ex-partner.

But Lee is not an abusive partner; he is my son, and with my support, and the support for both of us from our family and a therapist who specialises in helping children who have suffered from trauma, he is maturing into a loving and caring young man. He is still wary of new experiences and new people, he still needs to watch facial expressions and has to make sure I am not angry with him if I am not doing my "over the top smiley face" that I used when he was little to allay his fears of someone being hurt or hurting him.

**What was best?**

By far, best of all, is being a mum! But more than that it is being a mum and knowing that you have made a huge difference to a little boy who was getting too old and with too many issues for most would-be adopters. Our social workers often describe our family as "a success story", not because it's perfect but probably because I don't complain. In the early days, I'd just be rushing around and getting on with the day-to-day stuff, with no time to stop and think, and sometimes perhaps that's the best way. If you analyse everything, if you don't remember the good times when things get tough, then you get stuck in a negative cycle of not being able to see how far your children have come. Although progress might be little and slow, it's still progress. For us, progress was learning that Mum would sort it out, that the world doesn't end if something goes wrong, that Mum will still love me if I make a mistake. I'm really proud when people say to me, 'You've done great, he's a credit to you', because he is and I know that, but it's nice when other people see it too. I'm so proud of all that Lee has achieved and what he's overcome to get there.

The other best bit is that we've made lots of friends with adoptive families just like us, and that has been amazing for us. For me, because they offer the support and understanding that the professionals who don't "live" adoption cannot give, and for him, because he has all these friends 'just like me'. Although they don't

SECTION II

necessarily share their experiences, you can see their stature and confidence grow just by being together.

**The future**

Lee has just left school and is becoming increasingly independent, partly because he knows I am always there to help him. He still lives at home with me and will do for the long-term future. He is very emotionally intelligent and we have a caring and loving relationship. He knows he will have a home with me until he is ready to branch out on his own.

Lee is always going to need some measure of support, but I hope that it will lessen over time. He still needs guidance as he forgets to eat when he's busy, he needs to be reminded of the importance of eating breakfast to keep his blood sugar levels up or he will get crabby and irritable. He needs support with the other day-to-day stuff too, like wearing clean clothes, sorting out his money so he doesn't spend it all on "Minecraft", making his bed and tidying up after himself. But on the plus side he has learnt how to do minor repairs to his motorbike, how to make Mum a cup of tea to keep her onside, and he has gained some time management skills to get himself to places on time.

He still relies on me to use the telephone for him and to sort out insurance or bank details. Given the choice he would rather text as he can process the written word much more easily than speaking and then understanding what could be a long answer. His strategy is to put the phone on loudspeaker if he needs to use it so I can help him out if he doesn't follow what is asked of him.

My biggest hope for Lee's future is that he will find a

SECTION II

loving and caring girlfriend – he deserves that – and then I hope that he will sustain that relationship and not follow the route of his birth family and mine; that things don't turn "nasty" when they go wrong and that arguments don't lead to violence and the police being called. Then I will feel that ours is really a success story.

We are looking at college for next year and again I wonder how he will manage in a new environment and with new people without me being there to run to when he needs help or things are getting tricky for him.

In terms of his future employment I have concerns. Lee still struggles to interpret other people's attitudes and behaviour towards him. He will need a supportive employer who understands that he doesn't "get" jokes and feels put on the spot by expectations that he can do tasks that he looks capable of. For example, during his Compulsory Bike Training he clashed with the instructor who didn't understand that he needed a few minutes to gather himself, and perhaps phone me, before he felt confident enough to get out on the road on the motorbike. I wonder if there is an employer who will have sympathy with a grown man's dependence on his mother and not put it down to me being either overbearing or Lee being a "mummy's boy".

Lee's legacy of domestic violence is, in my opinion, the biggest problem he has to overcome or at least come to terms with. I know because I have also had to do it. He needs to be reassured about how people are feeling and responding to him; he still panics if I am not smiling, and even though he knows that doesn't necessarily mean I am angry, he still needs to ask. He has a heightened stress response and an assessment has shown that his moro reflex (responsible for the startle response in infants) is still present, which has disrupted his development. We have been given exercises to help with this, but he needs to be assessed again in six months.

The memory of domestic violence means that Lee has now asked me to stop letterbox contact with his birth parents. I have written every year and received letters back but now it's as if he's come to a point where his adoptive status doesn't define him any more. I've noticed that he hasn't told his sixth form that he is adopted, which at one time would have been one of the first things they would have known about him.

Would I do it again if I knew how it would be? Most definitely! It's been the hardest thing I have ever done in my life but also the most rewarding. Adoption has allowed us both to fulfil our hopes for the future, mine of being a mum and his of a "new mummy" who will keep him safe and love him forever.

**Golden rules**

So if I were asked what tips I could offer or what I would do differently, here's what I'd say:

- Read widely but also watch things like "Supernanny" and think about how you would do it differently because her strategies are not usually going to work with adopted or looked after children.

- Make sure you get as much information as you can about your child's background. It will help you to understand their behaviours.

- Don't listen to people who tell you 'all children do that' – they might, but not in the extreme way our children do!

- Watch your children whilst they are asleep – to see the true innocence on their faces and remind you that it's not their fault.

- Remember that it's not your fault either – you are doing your best in extreme circumstances sometimes.

- Get support from other adopters for all of you.

- Make the key person at school your best friend – a good school can make all the difference when the going gets tough.

- Work together with professionals – remember, they are trying to help.

- Believe in yourself – you are your child's best advocate.

- Find the good in every day – there is always a little bit in there.

- Be proud of your family.

SECTION 11

# Inviting in the storm

No child is ever too young to be damaged by domestic violence

**Melinda Rigopoulo**

It's seven o'clock in the morning and I am sitting on our balcony overlooking the valley below us, all of it hidden under a blanket of fog, with the mist rising off the river and the hills peeking out above it all. It's Sunday morning, private tea-time. This is my favourite part of the day, the calm before the storm, the time I should be using to do something worthwhile and life-prolonging like yoga or jogging or something useful like emptying the dishwasher. Instead, I sit, watch and listen. After a while, my son Luca, 14, comes upstairs and sits next to me. We've been enjoying the morning for a while in utter silence when he turns to me and says:

'Mum.'

'Mmmm.'

'I haven't had my morning hug.'

It's going to be a good day.

## How it all began

My husband and I had been wanting to adopt since before we knew each other, each for very personal reasons. When we first applied for a preliminary meeting to find out how to go about it, we were told we had no chance of being matched with a child as we were too young (mid-twenties) and fertile. We decided to start our family and adopt later; perhaps the child-care experience would make us better adoptive parents.

Eight years and two children later, we decided to re-embark on the adoption route. We welcomed the assessment process and felt it was good for us to be questioning our motivation and suitability and come out feeling either prepared or unsuitable. We came out feeling prepared. We had two lovely, healthy and happy birth children, knew friends and family who had adopted, and had a reasonable support system. I had read all the books about worst-case scenarios to really test whether we knew what we might be letting ourselves in for and to get an answer to the burning question of how this decision could affect our birth children.

We had been preparing our children for this step for some time, mentioning the topic casually now and again and discussing what this might mean for them. The usual spiel about sharing toys, being the big brother and sister, the chaos of a younger sibling, and the fact that he or she might not always be easy, or nice and might need the support of older siblings at times and personal space at others. I do believe that our birth children were as well prepared as any very young children can be. Our lovely and experienced assessment social worker Mandy thought so too.

I must admit that I did listen in to one of Mandy's assessment conversations with my son, who was four at the time and going through his 'I'm-the-dude' phase; I knew he was eager to impress anyone who would listen with his swagger. I just "happened to be passing" in the hallway when I heard her ask, 'So how would you feel about sharing your toys with a new child?' to which he responded, 'Yeah, that would be OK' (relief on my part). 'And what toy do you think you would want to show him or her?' (interest) 'My knife...I stole it from nursery.' I slunk away and suspected that might be the end of our assessment and the beginning of quite different social work involvement; Mandy mentioned this conversation later and we had a good laugh about it. Not much phased her.

Many times over the next few years, we were asked the big "W" questions: WHY had we chosen to adopt a traumatised child? WHAT were we thinking? The only honest answer I have ever been able to give to this question has been: 'Because it felt like the right thing.' Call it karma, destiny, fate, coincidence or just pure luck. So it came about that we adopted a bonny young lad of two with big brown eyes and a gorgeous smile: Enter Luca!

We didn't know much about him at the time except that he had been removed from the family at the age of six weeks following domestic violence and a non-accidental injury severe enough to put him in hospital. He'd been

69

with the same foster carers throughout: a very busy household with one adopted and five fostered children and several pets. We were told Luca was a happy, sociable child, a good eater and good sleeper but that he had global developmental delay as a result of his injury.

The foster carers were very supportive and co-operative during the introduction phase, which included an overnight stay at their house to get a feel for their daily routine on a 24-hour basis as well as multiple visits and a few day trips to our house to ease Luca in gradually. They even began adjusting his diet so our food would seem less strange when he came to live with us! They truly put children first in all they did. We vividly remember a videotape (good old VHS) the foster carers had made for potential adopters, which showed Luca in the family, at mealtimes, having his nappy changed, and one particularly impressive scene in which Luca and two other toddlers were crying at the same time, along with the dog who howled in solidarity. The scene deliberately lasts several minutes without intervention, with the foster carer commenting: 'And some days, this is how it can be. So I want your new parents to be prepared for this as well as your charm.'

**Coming home**

I distinctly remember the day Luca was brought to stay with us for good. We had insisted that he be brought by the foster carers to whom he had formed a good attachment. The aim was to avoid the "abduction scenario" to give him a sense that this was "right", although there is no doubt that it was still unsettling, confusing and frightening for him. Both foster carers arrived in their bus with a multitude of bags filled with clothing and a huge amount of toys. In order not to upset

Luca they left early, clearly struggling to hold back tears.

We have stayed in touch with the foster carers, with regular visits several times a year and we appreciate the obvious importance this relationship has for our son. Having said that, Luca's behaviour was always atrocious two days leading up to any visit and one to two days afterwards. As much as he enjoyed seeing them, he has always found each change to his routine unsettling and seemed to believe for a long time that they might, after all, be coming to take him back.

It was the same before any trip away, even if it was only for a day. It became clear that his need for safe surroundings, safe people and predictability was so great that each time we left home, he felt completely vulnerable and terrified. By acting out, he ensured that we kept him as close to us as physically possible during any journey, holding his hand and never letting him stray near his siblings, who didn't need to do much to set him off. What people *saw* was a "naughty boy", having tempers, swearing, hitting and kicking his parents till their equilibrium was seriously disrupted. What I *felt* was his terror, his fear of being lost or even deliberately left somewhere because he was so "bad". We rarely arrived at our holiday destination short of frazzled, exhausted and relieved. Luca always took several days to acclimatise to a new place; this was hugely helped by going on holiday to the same place for ten years, so he knew what to expect. The key things about holidays were:

- **Predictability:** we always had the same or similar routine.

- **Close proximity of sleeping quarters:** our rather

cramped holiday homes were great for always knowing where everyone else was, especially at bedtime.

- ***Water!*** We spent mornings and evenings on the beach, in the sand, in the water, returning home in the noon heat. The children played together or each at their own developmental level whilst we had them all in our field of vision and could take turns playing with them or sleeping! I may even have read a page or two of a book before one of them spotted me and came to relieve me of my "boredom": 'Poor Mummy, she's all alone. I'll play with you, Mummy!' Who could resist!

### Settling in

The early days, weeks, months and even years were hard work and extremely demanding, including, of course, for our birth children, especially my elder daughter, Theresa, who at nine seemed to think her role was one of co-parenting and co-responsibility for this cute but unpredictable little brother she had been blessed with. We did not see this straight away, but when we recognised the dynamics, we explained that she should not feel responsible for Luca but just enjoy him. Of course I was grateful for any support, but when she'd had enough or simply wanted to be on her own, I sent her to do her own thing and leave him to me. Years later, I asked Theresa whether she had ever resented Luca. Her response was healthy and insightful: 'Sure I did. I resented not being the centre of attention or having enough money to go on fancy holidays like some of my friends. But I felt the same about Alex (her birth brother) too, so it had nothing to do with adoption, just with sharing!' We had a good laugh and I hug her in my mind every time I think of this conversation.

Alex, aged seven, was more chilled about the added

chaos to his life. He would quite happily lie on the floor and play with Luca after school or spend hours trying to synchronise the music on the multitude of electronic toys he'd brought with him. The cacophony continued for weeks before I began to feel my sanity slowly slipping away. Miraculously, the batteries on all the toys gradually began to give out and we never seemed to remember to buy new ones. It transpired that Luca actually preferred the old-fashioned cuddly toys (non-talking or -singing!), wooden building blocks, toy cars accompanied by his very own rendition of various motor sounds, and the pleasantly taciturn dollies, all of which we had in abundance from our older children. He also loved stringing large beads (thank you IKEA!) and decorating us with the results or screwing together huge plastic cubes with oversized nuts and bolts to make little seats and boats in which his dolly-babies could go out and see the world. We had collected so many electronic toys, that eventually we had a very nice car boot sale to raise funds for the school's special needs department; one that Luca used himself in the years to come!

Once Luca had settled in he began catching up on his motor skills at an astounding pace! His speech also improved steadily under our family's "speech therapy"; we talked to him, commented on what we were doing, actively encouraged him to repeat words for objects but didn't force the issue and read to him LOTS! Television and computer time was non-existent. It would be fair to say that this approach is hard work, but we did also have our older children as eager story-readers and role models and children do seem to learn best from other children! All of this was worth it to see Luca coming on so well; a consolation for the fatigue that set in every single evening once all the children were in bed.

73

**Behaviour**

Luca had developed a very clever strategy for dealing
with his anxiety and fear of anything new or unknown.
Within his very limited vocabulary, the flavour of the
season was clearly the word 'No!'. He used this in
response to any and all questions or suggestions and
after some initial bafflement, we soon learned to read
between the lines.

Offered peas or pasta, his clear answer is: 'No.'

My husband, incredulous in view of the speed with which
both previous portions have been devoured, puts more
on his plate, which vanishes instantly. An offer of pudding
gets a clear: 'No.' Having gained in wisdom, we simply
place the pudding before him and he finishes off three
portions.

Pointing out the swings in the park, Luca clearly states
'No', hesitates, then runs towards them with a huge
smile of anticipation.

'Do you want to stroke the kitten?' 'No.'

'OK, I'll put her down then.' 'No!'

It became clear that 'No' was Luca 's way of stalling for
time whilst he tried desperately to discern:

- what it was he was being asked or offered and whether
  it was safe. In case it wasn't, 'No' would keep him on
  the safe side;

- whether this was something he could do, or whether
  he was bound to fail. 'No' protected him from failing by

protecting him from trying.

It was amazing over the years to see what a huge difference it made to Luca's self-esteem simply to be able to do normal things for himself that other children take for granted. The road to success, however, was very rocky and frequently interrupted by major temper tantrums at the first sign of failure. Dropping his spoon onto the floor by accident produced a look of shock and alarm on his face that was quite out of proportion to the event. We learned that we had to be extremely quick not only to retrieve the spoon but to distract him at the same time; otherwise, this tiny mishap brought a major meltdown in its wake. Luca would shout and scream, cry and throw other items onto the floor deliberately and was often so beside himself that we had to physically remove him from the table and sit with him in a quiet corner until he calmed down.

We obviously had experience of toddler tantrums, but there was a different quality to Luca's rage. It was painful to see him so very angry with himself for failing at any simple task, and he remained unreceptive to reassurance or praise for years. Luca simply did not hear praise, refused to believe he was good at anything, disbelieved us, his teachers and others that he had done well, and only remembered what had gone wrong or where he had failed. It took many years of constant and continuous positive reinforcement and refocusing on his strengths, achievements and talents before Luca ever began to believe he could be good at anything.

When it came to learning to ride a bike, Luca steadfastly refused to believe that he could, and every time he sat on the patient apparatus, he shrieked, 'No, I can't do it!'.

SECTION II

We calmly repeated countless times, 'Luca, you've already done it. I've seen you. You cycled all by yourself. And I'm here to catch you if you fall.' Many months later, and in the customary stooped position of parents administering cycling support, we watched our son hop onto that bike and whizz off. EVERYONE was over the moon over his success and we have had many similar cycles (no pun intended) of skill attainment since.

For Luca, the basic problem with attempting anything new is:

- the complete lack of self-confidence that he might succeed;

- the utter lack of frustration tolerance if he doesn't succeed immediately.

Anything new for Luca is subconsciously perceived as a potential threat. Instead of waiting to find out what it is he is meant to be doing, he gets restless, stops listening, and tries to find a way out. This behaviour is typical of children who have been traumatised by domestic violence; they may have been neglected or threatened, abused or frightened, or they may have sustained accidental or non-accidental injuries in response to their own signals of needing attention. As a newborn infant, Luca had probably experienced that whatever he did, it might be wrong and trigger negative or violent reactions from those adults closest to him; the ones he looked to for care and protection. As a result, he was continuously on edge and watchful. He only ever relaxed when he felt very safe; it must be absolutely exhausting to go through life on the constant lookout for danger!

As foster carers or adoptive parents, we often do not

have enough information about our children to know whether or not domestic violence is part of the picture, or whether the difficulties our children display are the result of other issues, such as learning or attachment difficulties, ADHD or physical injury. We had very little information about exactly what had gone on in the birth family prior to Luca being taken into care. We knew that there had been violence and that social workers were afraid to go into the house. It was likely from the history that there'd been violence in the birth family before the documented incident of injury. This would presumably have involved shouting, screaming and fear in Luca's birth mother. It is highly likely that this kind of stress in the home environment prevailed even before Luca was born, when he was in the womb. Non-accidental injuries rarely occur in isolation. It is sadly more common that minor episodes of violence escalate over time until the results become too obvious to hide, as in Luca's case.

Long-term continuous or recurrent exposure to high levels of stress hormones, whether before or after birth, interferes with the connections that are formed between the nerve cells within the brain. Once we understand how trauma may have affected a young brain's hard-wiring, the behaviour we see in our children suddenly makes perfect sense. It's all about survival.

A child's brain is programmed to achieve personal safety or survival. In response to trauma caused by domestic violence, the child is left with two alternatives to secure his or her safety:

- **Fight:** Rages that can be triggered even by minor events, or a low threshhold for stress in general, resulting in major meltdowns even years later.

- **_Flight:_** Dissociation, switching off from reality, often witnessed as daydreaming, freezing or trance-like states.

Luca's behaviour seemed irrational to others, yet it was elementary to survival from his own perspective. Having been neglected and left unfed and uncared for, subjected to shouting, threatening behaviour and actual injury, his brain had linked the violent behaviour of his carers to his own display of distress; whenever he cried he was either ignored or hurt. So later, when he felt uncomfortable or frightened, or was met with demands he felt he could not achieve (like learning something new), when he failed at a task or didn't know what was coming next, he took control over this frightening situation with his rage. Children who have experienced trauma before they had speech literally have no words to describe what happened, just the feelings. An infant's tools to protect himself are very limited. If the stress, pain or fear becomes unbearable, some infants simply take themselves away, switch off mentally and dissociate from what is happening to them. Luca had learned this survival tool as well.

As a young child, Luca's rages could be triggered not only by dropping a spoon, but also by having a picture go "wrong", sensing anxiety or irritation in someone close to him, or by having to wait for something to happen, which he found unbearable. We developed seismic sensitivity to when he was about to blow and needed distraction, cuddles, reassurance or a walk round the block. Like Luca, we also were in continuous alarm mode. This is exhausting and can secondarily traumatise the whole family.

When Luca was in a rage he could rarely be soothed, merely contained. We took him to a safe place, stayed by him, held him if he let us, and stuck it out. Talking in a low voice had a soothing effect and we often sang softly to him; gentle children's songs and lullabies, folk songs, blues, country, soul, we tried them all and they helped not only to bring him back down to earth, but also to control ourselves whilst being hit, scratched and kicked. If the cat walked in, he stopped almost instantly; her purring and the softness of her fur soothed him and he did not want to scare her off. Unfortunately, being a cat, she didn't come to order, but ran for it when Luca was too loud! Once calm, Luca immediately forgot the incident and acted as if nothing had happened. He had spent all his energy and played quietly for the rest of the day. Another approach that worked very well was getting him out of the house and doing something physical like raking leaves, taking a walk, riding his bike. Often, it was my husband who channelled Luca's anger into something constructive by spending quality time with him and replacing the anger, fear and negativity (*I am bad*) with a sense of achievement (*I am helpful and strong*).

In his rages Luca very often pushed us to the limit. It became increasingly clear that what he was trying to do was push us over the limit. He was so afraid of what might happen that he tried to provoke the violence he feared most, so he could relax when the worst had finally happened. On the occasions when he did get hurt at school or at home, even if by accident, his indignation and sheer distress at the fact that 'you HURT me!' was way out of proportion to the actual mishap. It was the existential insult to his very soul that distressed him, not physical discomfort.

SECTION II

79

Self-injuring behaviour began early with head-banging, slapping and pinching himself and threatening to throw himself out of the window. When he was nine, Luca walked across the room, opened the window of his second storey bedroom and sat on the window-sill threatening to jump. Deliberately keeping my distance I kept his attention on me: 'I don't think you really want to jump, you want a hug.' Pure auto-pilot, but I could see in Luca's eyes that the fact that he knew that I *knew* he wasn't really going to jump (did I?) gave him the sense of security and of being held that he had lost at that moment. As he shut the window, he turned to me and said, 'Why are you looking worried? You know I wouldn't really jump.' He went back to his playing and I was left feeling physically sick.

As a result of his trauma, Luca has extremely fine antennae. He will walk into a room and immediately sense if there is discord in the air, even if it has nothing to do with him directly. This state of hyper-arousal is part of his survival strategy and also his greatest vulnerability. To this day Luca is constantly looking for danger from others. He has never liked big groups, because he quite simply cannot keep abreast of everyone's emotional state at the same time, so his DANGER signals remain on. At 14, he is afraid of drugs and alcohol due to a fear of losing control; some youngsters do end up on drugs and alcohol because the stress of being constantly on the alert becomes unbearable. Luca's music teacher once told him to 'simply relax and enjoy the music'. Luca spontaneously responded: 'I can't relax. Ever.' The saying 'You snooze, you lose' has a very real and terrifying meaning for Luca, even after a decade of experiencing love, safety, personal success, popularity with peers and a sense of safety at home. To him the world outside truly is a jungle.

Luca is preoccupied with catastrophes, death and flashing lights and is obsessed with ambulances, rescue helicopters, police cars and accidents. Scenes from films or television at a friend's house cause him nightmares for weeks. He is preoccupied with the notion that a burglar might enter through his second storey bedroom window at night and hurt him. My pointing out that this burglar would need to be a combination of Spiderman and Flat Stanley is acknowledged by him rationally, but the window stays shut!

Luca has always had an intolerance of high sensory input, be it noise, light, lack of personal space, strong smells or spicy food. Particularly in the early days, one of his coping strategies in times of severe stress (loud classrooms, shopping malls, funfairs, bright lighting in shops) was to take himself away to somewhere else. You could see that he was not part of what was going on around him but focusing on one small activity to the exclusion of the rest of the world. The extreme form of this dissociation is absolutely heart-breaking to witness. When Luca was about six, another boy known for *his* rages, planted himself directly in front of him, and proceeded to shout at Luca so loudly that it could be heard across the playground. I watched Luca's facial expression change from sheer terror to a vacant stare and a frightening pallor in response to this overwhelming situation. I ran over and held him in my arms; he sat on my lap as stiff as a board, shaking like a leaf. It took several minutes for him to recover and he refused to go anywhere near the other boy for weeks.

SECTION II

81

### Education

At school, Luca has never ever had his rages. He's always said, 'I wouldn't dare. I'd be afraid of what might happen.' He was and is compliant, polite, friendly and very eager to please the teachers. He is, however, easily distractible and cannot take in the content of the lessons if anything new is introduced, such as a new teacher, a change of classroom or, as has unfortunately been the case for him, a change of schools. He is so busy studying the faces and behaviours of the teachers and other students to check that he is safe and that no one is suddenly going to lose their temper or do something unexpected, that he simply cannot take in the lessons as well. We have fought long and hard to find an inclusive school to meet his special educational needs, which are linked to his emotional state. He is now in a class in which he feels safe, happy and above all, normal. He is achieving good results with support, has friends and teachers whom he trusts, and he is less easily traumatised by unexpected events. He is now secure enough to actually learn, and he loves it (well, except maths...).

With his strong sense of justice he'll stand up for others, but needs constant reassurance that when someone does something wrong, there will be consequences. To this day, he needs this in order to feel safe. When he and a friend were recently approached indecently by an adult, his friend was too embarrassed to tell his mum about it. Luca told him 'My mum said that's wrong and that I should always tell an adult.' So they did; the advantage of black-and-white thinking. Wrong is wrong and must be righted. With Mum on the case, I can relax and trust that I am safe.

### What's it like for the others?

So what is it like for the adoptive family of children who have witnessed or experienced domestic violence?

#### For the parents:

- It is draining and potentially traumatising. You need strong support systems and a partner or close family to share the front line with you.

- Be prepared to doubt your parenting skills every day for years before you begin to see the fruits of your love, determined support and refusal to give up your child to its demons. Be a *good enough parent*, but be aware that there will be times when you will need to be *super parent* – and you'll do it too!

- We all know we cannot undo the hurt someone else has done to our child. But we still try and the children know it. It is immensely reassuring to know you have Mum or Dad on your side, no matter what.

- Parenting these children takes you to your limits and shows you things about yourself you might rather not know, but it will also unearth skills and a capacity for love that you never knew you had in you.

- You really MATTER to your child. If your child is an angel for everyone else and lets rip at home, this is because he/she feels safe enough with you to do so! And if he/she lets rip at school in order to get sent home to you, maybe this is telling you something too!

#### For the siblings

Living with a traumatised sibling is hard. We often worried about the effect the adoption might have on our birth children. Did they feel they'd grown through the experience or missed out? Our older two were well

SECTION II

adjusted, self-confident and securely attached children with good wits about them, good social skills and plenty of interests and talents. But they still needed their mum and dad. Being older, they occasionally wanted to do teenage things and have uncensored teenage conversations without the constraint of having a younger sibling around. They also needed to have one-to-one time with each of us and they needed to know that they mattered just as much, even if they were (usually) not as loud as their little brother! Through it all, neither of them has ever truly questioned our decision to adopt and when asked, they each lay claim to two siblings, no distinctions made.

I regularly accompanied my older children to sports competitions and national events, leaving Luca with my husband and vice versa. We all enjoyed that! When it became too much for Theresa, she'd leave to do her own thing, which was OK. Now she comes back from uni and looks forward to seeing Luca, being a part of his life and writing and receiving fantastic letters! Luca enjoys doing "big brother" things with Alex, like trips to the skate park, bike tours, discussing the football scores and debating the merits of pop songs on the radio.

I asked Theresa to write down what she remembers about living with Luca:

*Some of the first memories of living with him are how he loved to listen to the cat's purring; he would put his ear to its stomach, seemingly for hours. The feather duster and the vibration of the hoover were also favourites. As a ten-year-old, I didn't really understand why the tiniest things, like dropping his knife at dinner, would result in violent tantrums. To me he was an incomprehensible package of endearment, gentleness and sudden aggression. I was still a child and did not have an effective method for making sense of his behaviour, so I think I often reprimanded him harshly, which led to him hitting me every time I came into the room as all he expected from me was negativity. At the time, I was too overwhelmed to reflect on it much but in hindsight it saddens me that I did not possess the necessary insight into what he needed from me. His relationship with the world has, I think, improved over the years; however, it is clear that he will always bear the scars of his trauma. Helping him to cope with these in order to enable him to lead a fulfilling life remains a constant test alongside enjoying his company and wonderfully kind, humorous nature.*

**Survival tips for siblings:**

- It's great to help Mum and Dad, but don't become an additional parent. You're a kid, enjoy it!

- Have hobbies, enjoy your friends.

- Try to accept your sibling as he/she is and don't judge the behaviour as you would that of a friend. Remember he/she has been hurt; when you feel hurt, you sometimes feel angry at the world and often end up hurting the people closest to you. Don't take it personally. It's probably not you, but you can help by giving your sibling space and having fun with him/her when he/she has calmed down.

- Grab Mum or Dad on their own and play a game, work in the garden, go shopping or to the cinema, or whatever!

### Support, social services and friends

'Oh, how wonderful of you to adopt!' Whenever I heard that sentence I knew that I could expect no surprise visits for coffee from that person nor be invited to their summer barbecue. It was this awe and insecurity that kept many people away. My husband's memory of those early years is *isolation*. Our great thanks go to those friends who were there when we needed them, no questions asked. Whether offering to take one or more of our children along on outings or inviting us to a social event, we love you for it!

Despite being a high-risk placement, we were never seriously inconvenienced by visits from social workers. The children's worker came twice and then left the department. The replacement came 12 months later and hadn't even bothered to read the file before she came, which was a complete waste of our afternoon. Every bit of support had to be fought for by us, including the cost for Luca's therapy, which social services should have known would be on the horizon for us.

So finally, if you are brave enough to take on an emotionally hurt child, here are some tips.

### Tips for settling in your child

- **Take it slowly** and be prepared to stay at home with a pre-school child for at least one year. This year of bonding with your child and giving him/her a sense of a secure space in your family is time very wisely spent in view of the years ahead.

- **Spend lots of time** with your child. Don't let the TV have all the fun of entertaining him/her!

- **Don't send a young child to nursery soon after their arrival** unless it is one they already know well and feel secure in. Children *need to feel safe in your home* and family before they can feel safe elsewhere.

- **Be prepared to keep school-age children off school for a while if they need it.** The emotional security that a child gains through time spent at home after a turbulent history and a recent major move will help him/her to be able to cope at school. Sending a child to school too soon and having to pick him/her up three to five times a week when the school calls you is not nice for you or for the child. A new school means new surroundings, new teachers, new rules, new kids and all that before we even get to the curriculum! This is real stress for an emotionally wobbly child.

- **Keep the sensory input low and soothing.** Children don't need computers, TV or electronic toys. Try them with soft toys, toys made of natural materials, cushions, feathers, a sandbox, construction toys, and if possible a swing or a rocking chair – rocking soothes.

- **Reconsider before inviting all your friends**, the neighbours, Great Aunt June and her three dogs and the rest of your family over for a **welcoming party**. Your child is almost certain to be utterly overwhelmed by this. We had our first celebration a year into the placement and invited a few close friends who came and went throughout the course of a Sunday. It was lovely and relaxing and the children could play or join in as they chose.

- **Be prepared to work part-time** if your child isn't settling down after the first year. The time you spend with your child now is healing time that will reward you later!

- **Things DO get easier**, although it may take years.

**Survival tips for parents**

- **Expand your resources** using books (*The Boy who was Raised like a Dog*, by Bruce Perry, is a must!), or attend talks on trauma/attachment, and the educational needs of traumatised children.

- **Get help if you need it** and don't be afraid to ask; this includes *therapeutic support* for yourself or your child.

- **Get a life! Don't succumb to isolation.** Pursue a hobby, join a choir, meet up with a friend, get your nails done, go shopping or whatever turns you on. Once a fortnight is better than never. Invite someone over and don't tidy up!

- **5–15 minutes at the end of each day** or in between crises to have a coffee with your feet up is worth far more to your sanity than going out for a meal once every two months, when you are likely to fall asleep over the soup.

- **Don't lose sight of your partner or support person.** You are each other's best allies! Give each other breaks and be open about feeling overwhelmed and defeated when you do. Look at it this way: if you weren't doing such a grand job, it wouldn't feel so exhausting!

- **Stay true to yourself!** Be prepared to make compromises, but don't lose sight of your dreams.

- **ENJOY your children.** There are so many funny things that happen every day. Try to remember them, review the day at bedtimes (only the good things!) or keep a diary.

- **Reserve quality time for each child** already in the family.

- **If you have no family nearby, adopt a granny!** You will need your *support system*.

My son recently snuggled up to me and said: 'Ah, my mummy! I feel safe with you.' After all the things I am certain we did wrong, we must somehow have been *good enough parents* after all. This keeps us going!

I started with Luca and will let him finish. At 14, he is still easily uptight, but practises relaxation on his mum; from the depths of the armchair across which he is sprawled, his response to my admonitions regarding the state of his bedroom generates a drawn-out 'Aw, Mum, it's fine. Just chill!'

SECTION II

# References

Barron J (2007) *Kidspeak: Giving children and young people a voice on domestic violence*, Bristol: Women's Aid Federation

Brandon M and Lewis A (1996) 'Significant harm and children's experiences of domestic violence', *Child and Family Social Work*, 1:1, pp 33–42

Cavanagh K, Dobash ER, and Dobash RP (2007) 'The murder of children by fathers in the context of child abuse', *Child Abuse & Neglect*, 31:7, pp 731–746

ChildLine (1997) *Beyond the Limit: Children who live with parental alcohol misuse*, London: ChildLine

Cleaver H, Nicholson D, Tarr S and Cleaver D (2007) *Child Protection, Domestic Violence and Parental Substance Misuse: Family experiences and effective practice*, London: Jessica Kingsley Publishers

Cleaver H, Unell I and Aldgate J (2011) *Children's Needs – Parenting Capacity: Child Abuse: Parental mental illness, learning disability, substance misuse, and domestic violence*, London: The Stationery Office

Currie CL (2006) 'Animal cruelty by children exposed to domestic violence', *Child Abuse & Neglect*, 30: 4, pp 425–435

DeVoe E and Smith EL (2002) 'The impact of domestic violence on urban school children', *Journal of Interpersonal Violence*, 17: 10, pp 1075–1101

Fahlberg V (1994) *A Child's Journey through Placement*, London: BAAF

Fantuzzo JW and Lindquist CU (1989) 'The effects of observing conjugal violence on children: a review and analysis of research methodology', *Journal of Family Violence*, 4: 1, pp 77–94

Green H, McGinnity A, Meltzer H, Ford T and Goodman R (2005) *Mental Health of Children and Young People in Great Britain, 2004*, London: Office for National Statistics

Home Office (2013) *Domestic Violence and Abuse*, available at www.gov.uk/domestic-violence-and-abuse

Home Office (2014) *Strengthening the Law, Domestic Abuse Consultation: Summary of responses*, London: Home Office, available at www.gov.uk/government/

Humphreys C and Stanley N (2006) *Domestic Violence and Child Protection: Directions for good practice*, London: Jessica Kingsley Publishers

Joseph S, Govender K and Bhagwanjee A (2006) "'I can't see him hit her again, I just want to run away, hide and block my ears": a phenomenological analysis of a sample of children's coping responses to exposure to domestic violence', *Journal of Emotional Abuse* 16: 4, pp 23–45

McGee C (2000) *Childhood Experiences of Domestic Violence*, London: Jessica Kingsley Publishers

Mullender A, Hague G, Imam U, Kelly L, Malos E and Regan L (2002) *Children's Perspectives on Domestic Violence*, London: Sage

NCH Action For Children (1994) *The Hidden Victims: Children and domestic violence*, London: NCH Action For Children

Onyskiw JE (2003) 'Domestic violence and children's adjustment: a review of research', *Journal of Emotional Abuse*, 3:1/2, pp 11–45

Radford L, Corral S, Bradley C, Fisher H, Bassett C, Howat N and Collishaw S (2011) *Child Abuse and Neglect in the UK Today*, London: NSPCC

Perry B (2006) *The Boy who was Raised as a Dog*, New York, NY: Basics Books

Rutter M (1985) 'Family and school influences: meanings, mechanisms and implications', in Nicol RA (ed) *Longitudinal Studies in Child Psychology and Psychiatry*, Chichester: Wiley and Sons, pp 357–403

# Useful organisations

**The Anna Freud Centre**
12 Maresfield Gardens
London NW3 5SU
Tel: 020 7794 2313
www.annafreud.org

**British Association for Adoption and Fostering (BAAF)**
Saffron House
6-10 Kirby Street
London EC1N 8TS
Tel: 020 7421 2600
www.baaf.org.uk

BAAF is a membership organisation which aims to find secure, loving families for children who can no longer live at home and provides support and advice on all aspects of the adoption process. BAAF innovates, researches and co-ordinates a number of unique services and projects within the field of adoption. BAAF campaigns for the highest standard of child-centred policies and services, and is a key source of information, support and advice for professionals, adopters and the public.

### British Association for Counselling and Psychotherapy (BACP)

BACP House, 15 St John's Business Park
Lutterworth
Leicestershire LE17 4HB
Tel: 01455 883300
www.bacp.co.uk

### Caspari Foundation (formerly Forum for the Educational Therapy and Therapeutic Teaching, FAETT)

Gregory House, Coram Campus
48–49 Mecklenburgh Square
London WC1N 2NY
Tel: 02 7923 6270
www.caspari.org.uk

### The Centre for Child Mental Health

2–18 Britannia Row
London N1 8PA
Tel: 020 7354 2913
www.childmentalhealthcentre.org

### Family Futures CIC

3 & 4 Floral Place
7–9 Northampton Grove
London N1 2PL
Tel: 020 7354 4161
www.familyfutures.co.uk

## Post-adoption support

Your local authority has a duty to offer an adoption support service so you can always contact the appointed adoption support services adviser to see what is available. If they cannot help they will refer you to a specialist service. Many voluntary agencies also offer a post-adoption service. Below is a list of independent post-adoption centres.

### After Adoption Network

A group within Adoption UK to help adoptive parents share information and support. To join the network you must be a member of Adoption UK. As a member you will receive a list of adoptive families in the network who you contact through meetings or by telephone.

**Adoption UK**
Linden House
55 The Green
South Bar Street
Banbury
Oxfordshire OX16 9AB
Tel: 01295 752240
**www.adoptionuk.org.uk**

**After Adoption**
Head Office
Unit 5, City Gate
5 Blantyre Street
Manchester M15 4JJ
Actionline: 0800 056 8578
**www.afteradoption.org.uk**

**After Adoption Yorkshire**
Hollyshaw House, 2 Hollyshaw Lane
Leeds LS15 7BD
Tel: 0113 230 2100 (Mon, Tues, Thurs and Fri 10am–1pm,
and Wed, 4–7pm)
Email: info@aay.org.uk
**www.afteradoptionyorkshire.org.uk**

**Post Adoption Centre (PAC)**
5 Torriano Mews
Torriano Avenue
London NW5 2RZ
Advice line: 020 7284 5879
Mon, Tues and Fri 10am–4pm, Wed–Thurs 2–7.30pm
**www.pac-uk.org.uk**

**Parents and Children Together (PACT)**
7 Southern Court
South Street
Reading RG1 4QS
Tel: 0300 456 4800
Email: info@pactcharity.org
**www.pactcharity.org**

**Post-adoption LINK** (run by Barnardo's)
Covering Bedfordshire, Cambridgeshire, Essex, Hertfordshire, Norfolk,
Peterborough, and Suffolk
Tel: 01206 362540 (Mon–Fri 9.30am–4pm)

**Women's Aid Federation of England**
PO BOX 3245
Bristol BS2 2EH
Tel: 0117 9444411
Email: info@womensaid.org.uk
National Domestic Violence Helpline: 0808 2000247
(available 24 hours a day)
www.womensaid.org.uk

## WALES

**After Adoption**
Actionline: 0800 056 8578
www.afteradoption.org.uk

## SCOTLAND

**Birthlink**
21 Castle Street
Edinburgh EH2 3DN
Tel: 0131 225 6441
www.birthlink.org.uk

**Scottish Adoption Support Service**
Suite 5/3, Skypark SP5
45 Finnieston Street
Glasgow G3 8JU
Tel: 0141 248 7530
Email: sass@barnardos.org.uk
www.barnardos.org.uk